Horace Sumner Tarbell

**A Teachers' Manual of Lessons in Language**

Horace Sumner Tarbell

**A Teachers' Manual of Lessons in Language**

ISBN/EAN: 9783743417199

Manufactured in Europe, USA, Canada, Australia, Japa

Cover: Foto ©Paul-Georg Meister /pixelio.de

Manufactured and distributed by brebook publishing software (www.brebook.com)

Horace Sumner Tarbell

**A Teachers' Manual of Lessons in Language**

A

# TEACHERS' MANUAL

OF

# LESSONS IN LANGUAGE.

BY

HORACE S. TARBELL,

SUPERINTENDENT OF SCHOOLS, PROVIDENCE, R.I.,
AUTHOR OF LESSONS IN LANGUAGE.

BOSTON, U.S.A.:
GINN & COMPANY, PUBLISHERS.
1892.

# MANUAL

TO

## TARBELL'S LESSONS IN LANGUAGE.

### INTRODUCTION.

IN this introduction will be found certain suggestions that are applicable to several grades of pupils.

Those suggestions and details of work which are particularly designed for a single grade follow this introduction and are arranged in chapters whose titles designate the grade to which they are applicable.

By pupils of the first grade are meant pupils of the lowest grade, or first school year.

The name of the grade, as used in this book, corresponds, in all cases, with the number of the year of school work.

The allotment of this work to the several years — first, second, and third — is not intended to prevent more or less being done by classes than is here laid down; but to form an approximate standard of progress, and to indicate the order in which the work is best accomplished. Classes of higher grades must often review the work of lower grades. When a subject, already partially treated, is to be taken up anew, it will usually be best to begin with a review of the work already done in this subject.

There are two lines of work — oral and written — that must be carried on simultaneously almost from the first.

The oral work leads to the formation of a working vocabulary, and to the ability to use it, in accordance with good usage, in the construction of sentences.

When the child enters school his vocabulary consists of names for things, words to denote quality, action, relation, manner, place, etc., and he usually has the power to combine these in sentences to express his judgments. It is the duty of the teacher to revise and extend this vocabulary, until it shall cover all the fundamental forms of thought. This is best done by conversational lessons that recall observations, and lead to further exercise of the pupil's senses, through which alone come his conceptions.

Marcel says: "An enlightened teacher can always draw out his pupils by questioning them on the forms, colors, dimensions, and other properties of any article whatever; on its value, origin, mode of fabrication, and on the substances which enter into its composition. By the relations which this article may bear to others, he will be led to conversing with them on a great number of things, which cannot fail to extend their vocabulary and enlarge the sphere of their ideas."

The second and, after a time, parallel work is to give the pupil the ability to *write* the sentences expressing his thoughts.

To gain this ability certain steps are helpful.

*First*, to copy script.

*Second*, to copy print in script form.

*Third*, to write from memory.

*Fourth*, to write from dictation.

*Fifth*, to learn the use of capitals and marks of punctuation, and become familiar with customary forms of various papers or documents.

These are items of technical knowledge pertaining to the written forms of composition, and their mastery will enable one to express himself with the same readiness with his pen as with his tongue.

The oral process must, in all cases, precede the written, as being simpler, readier, and less difficult.

The first four of the steps enumerated above can be taken best under the eye and inspired by the voice of the teacher. It is a mistake to put a book on language into the hands of the pupil at this stage of his progress.

Of the fifth step not much can be taken without the need of a text-book being seriously felt.

The art of composition itself may be quite independent of the pen, and at first proceeds best without it; for the child thinks in spoken words, and puts his thoughts into written words only by a process of translation.

Later in life, if he practise composition much, he thinks directly in written words, — as one learns to think in French after considerable study of the language, — and then the pen becomes an important aid to composition.

The conversational exercises designed to increase the number and distinctness of the pupil's concepts, and to give him a knowledge of the words which are their signs, may be considered *language lessons* or *object lessons*, according as they are viewed from their formal or their material side.

Language must have a place in the daily school programme, and must also receive attention in all school exercises. In the time of the regular language lesson the pupils learn what to say and how to say it; but in all their exercises their habits of speech are in process of formation, and must be continually guarded.

## THE LESSONS

in this Manual are so framed as to secure from the pupils the use of the essential forms of common speech. If the children use these forms readily, through the influence of cultured homes or of previous instruction, the class passes at once to the next topic of instruction. With uncultivated and untrained children the questions in these exercises will occasion the thoughts which the teacher desires to have expressed; but the proper form of expression may not be within the pupils' power. In such cases, — and they will be many, — the proper answer must be substituted by the teacher, and the child be required to repeat his answer in the proper form. The child is to be stimulated to mental activity and free expression. He must be led to form the habit of good expression, so that he will try to say in precise and accurate language just what he thinks.

Incomplete and inaccurate sentences should be rejected, and good answers should receive judicious commendation. A very good answer may sometimes be written upon the board by the teacher or by the pupil who made it. This serves the double purpose of affording commendation and presenting a model.

## GENERAL METHOD.

When a new topic is taken up, it should be dwelt upon until thoroughly understood by the class. This will usually require a full lesson, and often two, three, or four lessons. This point being gained, the teacher should advance to the next topic, and so proceed, in regular order, through the course for the year, or grade. When a topic is first taken up, if it be at all difficult, the entire time of the lesson in language should be given to it; but, usually with the second and subsequent lessons on a given topic, some review work, increasing daily in amount until the next topic is taken, can be done. This review work should consist usually of two parts: first, a continuation of the work upon the preceding topic; second, a more remote review which begins with topic one, and continues until it overtakes the advance work. The remote review should then commence once more near the beginning of the work, and so on continually. In the later reviews, topics upon which sufficient attention has been bestowed can be passed over as the review proceeds.

The lesson will thus usually consist of three parts: the advance work, the near review, and the remote review.

Probably the first exercise of the morning and of the afternoon session will be found most advantageous for this work. All should participate.

In new work, the bright, quick pupils should be called upon first, and the slower ones later.* In review work, this order should usually be reversed, but none should be neglected. After the first two years a single daily exercise will be sufficient.

## TIME REQUIRED.

Training children to use well their mother tongue will require much time and effort from the teacher. Much more than in any other school work will skill in questioning be required. Many of the questions which the teacher proposes to ask must be formulated in advance with great care and either committed to memory or copied into the recitation note-book. Success will demand an immense amount of drill and iteration. Day after day, week after week, month after month, must the teacher continue the work of establishing the habit of using this and that acceptable form of speech.

Do not fear that it will be monotonous to the children. If you prepare yourself with care every day the work will never be wearisome to your pupils, but pleasant rather, because a sense of growing skill and power will give them delight. And yet a caution is advisable. A series of similar questions, involving no effort to answer them, may become tiresome. Only thought-compelling questions or those directly preparatory to such should ever be asked in the recitation.

## DICTATION.

Dictation is an exercise whose importance cannot well be overrated. Not much original written work should be attempted until the pupil has had considerable dictation drill.

Before dictation is attempted the pupil should have practice in copying script from the blackboard and print from a text-book. Next, the pupil should write from memory verses, maxims, and gems until he obtains readiness in the use of the pen.

While this practice is in progress the pupil should gain some knowledge of the fundamental rules of punctuation, of capitals and paragraphing, from having his attention called to these elements in that which he copies.

The teacher should make herself sure by test and explanation that the meaning and spelling of every word in the sentences to be dictated are known by the pupils before they are set to writing them.

The first dictations should be of matter which had been copied some time before. These dictations should be followed by those of new matter, quite similar in form to the previous ones.

This work is particularly adapted to the second and third years of school life, and should occupy a large percentage of the time allotted to language lessons during these years. If it be carried on in an order duly progressive and with sufficient painstaking, an admirable foundation for future progress will be laid.

A dictation exercise may be conducted as follows : The class being ready with slates and pencils at hand, but not in hand, the teacher reads through the paragraph which is to be dictated, pupils listening but not writing. The teacher then reads again the paragraph, a few words at a time, and pauses at the end of each reading to give the class time to write the words read. When the paragraph is in this way completed, the teacher may reread it continuously as was done at first.

After the dictation, have the exercise written correctly upon the blackboard. (If this could be done before the lesson and could remain covered from the sight of the children it would be better.) Let each pupil then compare his own work with the board work and make the necessary corrections.

If the exercise is not new or specially difficult, instead of correcting from the blackboard, papers may be exchanged for correction and the teacher may then reread the dictation, naming the points to be noticed.

## ORAL DESCRIPTIONS.

The child's first descriptions will, of course, be oral, and likewise brief and partial. They should be of things in which he is interested, and about which he desires to tell others. A child may be sent to the window and after taking his seat may tell of one or of several things that he saw, describing them so as to picture them to his mates. Perhaps he saw a tree. Let him so describe it that the others will recognize it. Perhaps he saw a man in a carriage. Let him give such items respecting the man, the horse, the carriage, as will convey some definite idea. He may describe, without naming it, something that he saw on his way to school, and the class may tell what it is.

## CHILDREN'S GAMES.

The games of children furnish good material for language work. Ask the children what games they know how to play; how many can play each game. Have some child tell the rest how it is done. If it be a game for the house let several of the children play the game, the rest looking on and thinking how to describe it.

After the game is over have several of the children describe the game as it was and as it should be played, giving the good points noticed and criticising the mistakes or neglect of the players.

Such a topic makes a good subject for oral, but not for written, composition, except with pupils older than we are now considering. Such a topic will afford a convenient opportunity to give the children the idea of orderliness in description.

## NARRATION.

Narration concerns itself with events; description, with things. Narration uses verbs and adverbs as description uses nouns and adjectives. The study of narration begins with personal experiences, continues through stories, heard or read, fables, and biographies, to history, which is the highest form of narration.

For an early exercise in narration, encourage children to tell what they did last evening after school, this morning before coming to school; what they did on Saturday last; what they did in the last vacation. Children should be encouraged to tell their mates of the things they have seen and heard. The desire to tell should give zest to expression. In the effort to interest others in their discoveries real composition can be secured without drudgery. Every night tell the little ones to find out something for the next day, and in the morning have a conversation exercise based on the children's own discoveries.

## ORAL REPRODUCTION.

One of the best tests of a trained mind is the ability to reproduce a story accurately and fully. One of the best exercises in language training is reproduction. Reproduction is of thoughts, not of words nor of sentences.

For a child to be able to give readily and in good language the substance of what is told to him or of what he reads is an attainment of great value. His career as a pupil depends very largely upon the possession of this power.

Teachers usually try to train their pupils in this direction, but many fail because they do not attempt it wisely or with sufficient preparation. The child will reproduce better what he hears than what he sees; narration than description. Hence stories told to the children should be selected for the first reproductions. (*a*) The work may be commenced by asking each child to tell a little story to the class, beginning with the children most forward and apt in this work, and continuing until all or nearly all have told two or more stories. (*b*) The teacher may tell short and interesting stories to the class, and have them repeated on the following day by several of the children. Fables, anecdotes, biblical and classical stories are suitable for this purpose. The story should be very interesting and long enough to prevent the pupils from remembering the exact words of the teacher, but not too long to have the incidents all recalled by the greater part of the pupils. It will do no harm to repeat the same stories over again after a few weeks. (*c*) The teacher may read a little story, stopping at the end of each phrase and sentence to give the explanations which seem necessary. There should be an animated and interesting conversation in which the children should take the larger part; but the thought and form should be directed by the teacher. "Do not talk to the children, but with them. The child is, above all things, active, and this activity should be afforded full opportunity to display itself." It is not so much you who are to talk with the children as the children who are to talk with you. The explanations finished, the teacher will read the story a second time from beginning to end without interruption, and will then have it repeated from memory by several of the children, letting the other pupils supply any omissions or correct any misstatements. The story may be repeated on other days by other pupils until it can be told readily by any of the class.

## WRITTEN REPRODUCTIONS.

Written reproductions should not be attempted until the class has reached a fair degree of facility and of correctness of expression in oral reproductions.

Oral expressions can readily be put into better form, if need be, through the suggestions of the teacher before crudities of expression have become fixed as they would be by the use of the pencil.

It is fortunate that when we express ourselves in oral language, intent chiefly upon the thought, as we always ought to be in a first expression, the language that we use makes very little impression upon us, and we are not very likely to recall it. But if we write, the slowness and formality of the writing and the sight of the words in their order in the sentences, tend to fix the words and their arrangement in the mind. Hence, expressions should be put into the best form readily obtainable by the pupil, before they are committed to writing.

METHOD. After a story has been reproduced orally, and before it has become familiar by repetition, the teacher may write upon the board a little summary of the story or a column of catch words that will help the pupils to reproduce the story. The pupils may then be set to writing it, each in his own style, but fully and interestingly. During this writing the teacher may pass among her pupils to notice their work, giving an occasional suggestion or criticism, or she may stand by her desk ready to answer questions as to the spelling of words, the punctuation of sentences, or the best forms of expression.

When the time for writing has expired, all should be required to cease writing and to attend to the reading and criticism of what they have written. As they read, one after another, their reproductions, these may be criticised by the teacher or by the pupils as to (1) omissions, (2) incorrect statements, (3) faulty constructions.

Omissions should be supplied by other members of the class. Incorrect statements should be rectified and faulty constructions amended during a free and kind conversation between teacher and pupils.

It is not necessary that the teacher should look over the slates or papers for minute criticisms. The reading will suggest the main points.

The teacher of younger pupils may ask, What is your first sentence? How does it begin? How is it punctuated? How are the words spelled? Can it be improved? Appeal to the class to know if the answers are correct.

Exercises not well done should be rewritten. Young children are much more patient of these rewritings than older ones are, and all of the simpler and more common faults of writing ought to be extirpated at an early period.

### GEMS.

Pupils from their first attendance at school to their entrance to the high school should learn every week some line, stanza, or paragraph, beautiful in thought and in language.

At first the sentiment, the moral influence of the passage, should be chiefly considered; but later the beauty and the force of the language and the breadth and the truthfulness of the thought must be regarded. For the first half dozen years of school life, all in a class should learn the same passages and recite them individually and in concert, receiving such paraphrase and explanation as may lead the pupils to get the thought and appreciate its dress.

Selections to be memorized are not included in this book, for much will depend upon the taste and must be left to the choice of the individual teacher. The sources of such gems as may suit the taste of all are not far for any one to seek.

### DESCRIPTION OF PICTURES.

A favorite exercise with teacher and pupils is the description of pictures. This cannot well be done before the second year. Some

## DESCRIPTION OF PICTURES.

preliminary training is requisite to prevent the description from becoming mere talking with little thought, or the dull repetition of a form. Monotony is proof of bad method. Before pupils undertake the description of pictures they need preparatory lessons in describing position, form, size, color, and quality. The forms "I see," "there is," "he has," and others, with their plurals and the present and past tenses of several verbs such as are needed in describing actions, must also be taught.

The teacher's platform or the corner of the room in front of the pupils may constitute the frame of the first pictures to be described, and the children themselves, variously posed, may represent the pictures. This will awaken interest, secure thought and free expression, give endless variety, and accord with the order of the child's mental development.

Position is one main element to be described in a picture. A good drill upon description of position may be given by placing two or three boys before the school in certain relative positions which the pupils describe. Vary these positions and secure the appropriate changes in the description.

A very simple arrangement might be described as follows: "On the platform are two girls, Mary and Ellen. Mary is older than Ellen, and is sitting in a chair, while Ellen is standing at her right side a little in front of her. Ellen is holding out a book to Mary. I think she will let Mary take the book to study her lesson."

This is more than enough for the younger pupils to say at first, but as they become expert at description they can describe, more minutely, the girls, their dress, their attitude, their purpose, their actions, etc.

Various articles may be made accessory to the main features of the scene, as the desk, the blackboard, the cabinet, the doors, the windows, the pictures upon the wall.

A definite understanding of the extent of the picture should be given in advance. The teacher may enter the scene, acts may be performed, and little tableaux arranged, as the skill of the pupils in description increases.

The following hints of simple arrangements that can readily be varied and improved by any apt teacher, are given to suggest the resources for this work found in any school-room: —

1. A child with her doll, which she is teaching to walk (dance).
2. Teacher holding in her lap a little child, who . . .
3. A boy, with two others as his horses.
4. Boy playing doctor to the doll of a little girl.
5. Two boys, with hats and canes.
6. Girl with basket on arm.
7. Boy with express-wagon.
8. Teacher pointing to an example on the blackboard, at which three boys are looking.
9. Little girl arranging teacher's desk.
10. Ditto, two girls . . .
11. Boy holding another by the hand.
12. Small boy teaching a class.
13. Pupil writing on the board, another sitting in the teacher's chair reading.
14. A little girl showing a smaller boy pictures in her book.
15. Two boys leaning over a table drawer.
16. A boy helping a little girl down from the platform.
17. Five children dancing in a ring.
18. One girl putting flowers into another girl's hair.
19. Two girls seated, with their dolls.
20. Two boys shaking hands.
21. Boy leaning on the back of an empty chair.
22. Boy leaning on the chair in which another is seated.
23. A girl showing another something in a basket.
24. Two girls, with arms around each other's necks, pointing to a girl on the other side of the platform.
25. Boy and girl, with skates in their hands.
26. Two boys, one with skates in his hands, the other with books.
27. Two boys come upon the platform from opposite sides, meet, shake hands, and pass off.
28. A child with eyes shut and mouth open, another putting something into the open mouth.
29. Two children with hands clasped high, a third creeping under their hands.
30. A boy giving a girl some flowers.
31. Two boys swinging their caps.

## METHODS WITH PICTURES.

Many sets of pictures suitable for this work are now published, or the teacher can make her own. Some gray cardboard cut to suitable size, a paste-brush, paste, and scissors will furnish the "plant." Publishers' catalogues, the illustrated papers, juvenile picture books, the card stores, etc., etc., will furnish the pictures. The children will readily bring many of them from home.

Large pictures easily seen by one entire class may be mounted on manilla paper, with eyelets attached for suspension.

A picture may be placed before a class for study and description, and such words as would naturally be used in the description may be placed upon the blackboard. These words become suggestive to the children, who weave them into sentences descriptive of the picture.

If a sufficient number of pictures can be obtained, they may be distributed to a division of pupils, who arise and each in turn describe the pictures which they hold.

In describing pictures, the actual size of the objects represented should be stated, and, as far as practicable, illustrated. This will prevent many unfortunate misconceptions and develop the picturing power of the mind.

A picture may be studied at several successive lessons, receiving each day a new treatment. The first day the objects may be noted and names given. For another lesson the qualities of the objects may be, as far as possible, determined. Next may be considered the relations of the parts of the picture to each other, the position, what they are doing, why so doing. Some story of which this picture might be an illustration may become a fourth exercise. In most cases, however, it will be better to proceed more rapidly than this.

*Teacher.* What do you see in this picture?
*Pupil.* I see a little boy.
*T.* What is the boy doing?
*P.* He is carrying in his right hand a tin can, under his left arm a loaf of bread wrapped in a brown paper, in his left hand a basket containing corn and beans.
*T.* Where has the boy been?

*P.* I suppose he has been to the grocery on some errands for his mother.
*T.* What kind of boy do you think that he is?
*P.* I think that he is an industrious and obliging boy.
*T.* Yes; he rose early this morning, to do some chores and go to the store before he went to school. Can you now tell about this picture without my questions?
*P.* I see in this picture a little boy who, etc.
*T.* You may write something about this boy. See what you can write in ten minutes.

It may be well to take the same picture, a day or two later, and encourage each pupil either to expand and improve his former effort or to give an entirely different treatment.

When a class has gained sufficient skill in the work, the following general form for the description of pictures may be suggested: (*a*) What is in the foreground, the background, at the right, at the left? (*b*) The persons or things that are to be seen; what are their names, acts, characters, appearance? (*c*) Invent a story to correspond with the picture.

## ILLUSTRATIVE PICTURES.

For pupils of the third and higher grades, the following exercise will be found very useful, if the class has sufficient talent therefor. Some pupils in every class will be able to succeed surprisingly well in such exercises.

The teacher selects some paragraph from the reading lesson, and, after it has been read by the class, says: "Each of you imagine the scene about which you have read and tell how it looks to you. If you were to paint a picture to illustrate this scene, what would the picture be? Describe it to us so that we shall see the picture that you do."

## CORRECTION OF WRITTEN WORK.

Doubtless every teacher will have her own plan for the correction of written work. Yet some of the following suggestions may be helpful: —

First, prevention is better than correction. Instruction should precede written work and prepare for it. See note 2, p. 211, Book I.

Mistakes in spelling require special, early, and persistent treatment. The pupils' written exercises should furnish the material for a considerable portion of the spelling lessons of the class.

At the time of writing, pupils should be encouraged to ask the teacher how to spell any word which they wish to use and which they do not feel sure they know how to spell.

As pupils read their written work they may be asked about the spelling of certain words, their use of capitals and marks of punctuation. Thus these three elements of error may be considerably eliminated from the papers before they are handed to the teacher.

The papers of the class should lie upon the teacher's desk from the close of one written exercise to the beginning of the next, and during this time the teacher should look them over sufficiently to discover how well they are done and what the more common errors are.

At the beginning of the next lesson in language these papers may be handed to the class, each pupil receiving the paper of some one else, and mistakes may be marked.

Words misspelled should be underscored. Errors or omissions in the use of capitals and marks of punctuation may be shown by P placed at the beginning of the line in which the mistake appears. The sign V placed at the beginning of a line may signify that in this line there is some mistake other than in spelling, capitals, and punctuation.

Papers may then be returned to the writers, and each pupil may write upon a slip of paper the words misspelled, and upon his slate, in amended form, the sentences in which errors were found.

If a pupil has any doubt about the correction of a marked sentence let him show it to the teacher, or copy it upon the board for the consideration of the class and the teacher.

The pupil making most mistakes in spelling should collect the slips containing the several misspelled words, and copy the words upon the blackboard. These words should be studied and used later in a spelling or dictation exercise. After such an exercise all words that no pupil has misspelled may be erased and the rest may remain for further study.

It will not do, however, to make the search for mistakes in spelling, punctuation, and grammar the chief effort of the class critics. After these things have been sought out and marked, let the critics next look for sentences or constructions for which they can suggest improvement, and for omissions which they can supply. Finally, let them seek for points of excellence which deserve commendation. Usually, two or three of the better exercises should be copied upon the blackboard, and the elements that render them praiseworthy be pointed out.

## CORRECTION OF ORAL ERRORS.

Training to correct speech has a positive and a negative side.

This manual and the books it accompanies set forth the positive side, which consists, speaking broadly, of furnishing the occasion for the use of correct forms of speech and assisting pupils to develop the power of using these forms. The negative side demands the exclusion from the language of the child of erroneous or inelegant forms, unconsciously imitated from the speech of those about him.

Incorrect language should be corrected whenever heard, not perhaps at the moment of utterance, for by so doing the child may be embarrassed and his current of thought broken, but at the first convenient opportunity. Besides this incidental correction, a wholesale crusade against bad habits of speech must be entered upon. The most common and serious fault in the speech of the children should be selected for special attack. The better form should be presented in contrast and made prominent. The pupils should be warned against this error in their own speech and led to criticise it in others.

It is not necessary to explain the grammatical or rhetorical principles which prove the expression to be a faulty one, but the form to use instead should be carefully explained and always insisted upon.

Professor W. D. Whitney says, "If a child comes to school in such a state of training that he says *come* for *came*, *done* for *did*, or *them* for *they*, and the like, he needs to be corrected outright, and the more authority and the less grammar about it the better."

## CHAPTER I. — FIRST YEAR.

The objects of lessons in language for the first school year are: —
(1) To secure to the pupils freedom in talking.
(2) To secure correctness in talking, which involves
    (*a*) a knowledge of common forms of speech, and
    (*b*) the avoidance of common errors.
(3) To enlarge the child's vocabulary and teach him to connect thought and speech.

To secure freedom in talking will require, on the part of the teacher, a pleasant manner and a gentle persistence in drawing the children out in conversation. Suitable topics of conversation are those that the child is interested in, knows something about, and can readily make the subjects of some statements or questions.

The lessons on form, color, qualities, and number, of the first year, are all available for language training.

The new words taught may be used in original sentences by the pupils.

The animals with which the children are familiar, those named and described in the reading book, and those of which good specimens may be seen, or of which good pictures may be shown, may form the basis of descriptions.

The transition from home to school should not be made abrupt and startling. The newcomer should be welcomed by his fellow-pupils and above all by his teacher with gentleness and helpfulness.

The first day, and for successive days, there should be conversations with the children connecting their school life with their home life. The pupil should be taught to recognize the many things in the schoolroom that he has known at home: the windows, the doors, the floor, the ceiling, the chairs, the clock, the cups; then things common in name, but different in style: as the table, the bookcase, the thermometer; then the different things: the blackboard, the desks, the crayon, the pointers, the erasers.

The name of the article in a correct sentence is all that should be called for at first.

The older children may be called upon to instruct the younger, to tell them the names of the articles in the schoolroom, to describe the exercises of the school to them. The method might be: One of the oldest and most intelligent of the pupils might take one of the youngest by the hand and lead him about the schoolroom, telling him the names and uses of the articles which they find: as, this is a desk, this is an eraser, etc. This younger pupil might, in his turn, point out each article and repeat what he has been told, his classmates in their seats observing and correcting. The teacher, in conducting this exercise, should insist on correct forms of speech and complete sentences being used by the pupils. Such an exercise may be continued until its utility is gone.

These exercises will incidentally teach the use of *this* and *that*, *a* and *an*, *is* and *are*, with many common forms of speech.

### Pupils' Answers.

The first errors to be corrected will be gross mispronunciations and the tendency to ellipses, or incomplete sentences.

The idea of the sentence is really the first objective point in language teaching. Pupils may sometimes be allowed to answer questions by the use of single words, when it is most natural to do so; but a question should usually be so framed as to draw out a sentence for its answer.

ILLUSTRATION. *Teacher.* How many hands have you?
*Pupil.* Two.
T. Tell me more about it. "Two" is only part of the answer I want. Say "I have two hands."
P. I have two hands.
T. How many feet have you?
P. I have two feet.
T. How many fingers have you on one hand?
P. I have four fingers on one hand.

*T.* What is there on the table?
*P.* There are some books on the table.

Continue such work until the pupils gain the idea of the form of answers that is required and acquire the habit of giving such answers. You will have no success in teaching language until this habit is established.

### *This is.*

When the children are at their ease in their new surroundings, the desire to use their senses, to do, and to talk, should be afforded gratification.

Place in the pupil's hands some object, or tell him to get it. Let him show it to the school and tell what it is. He will say: This is a knife; this is a spool; this is a string, etc. Let many pupils do this until all have confidence to walk quietly and quickly to the platform, to turn politely to the school, and to name distinctly, in full sentences, the objects.

### *This* AND *That.*

The form *this is* having become familiar, and the names of many objects being readily given, the pupils may be taught to distinguish between *this* and *that.*

The little fellow may hold up his toy, as before, and say: This is a ball. The teacher, holding in her hand a walnut, says: Tell me what this is. The pupil says: That is a walnut. Continue this with many objects. Have a pupil stand upon the platform and let his classmates in various parts of the room name the objects which he exhibits. Let the pupils in their seats in their turn hold up objects for him to name, which he does by saying: That is a spool; that is a rake; that is a top; that is a spade; that is an acorn; that is an eraser.

The teacher will find a box of little iron toys very convenient for this work.

### A DEVICE.

A device to secure attention and afford variety:—

The teacher may place in a box, bag, or other receptacle, a variety of articles familiar to the pupils by sight. Then, while the children, with the teacher, sing the following little song, a pupil, with eyes closed, may take out one or more articles and hold them behind him. At the end of the song, holding the article up to view, he may name it, saying : This is ———.

" While we're playing to geth - er  We are hap - py and glad,
Now    tell    lit - tle pla"mate What you hold in your hand,

We don't care for the weather, And we'll nev - er   be   sad.
And    if   you guess rightly,  We will clap  as   you stand."

Many devices can be found in books and magazines for kindergartners, which can readily be adapted to primary work.

### THE USE OF *a* AND *an*.

By showing suitable objects in the manner indicated under the topic *this* and *that*, such statements may be secured as: This is an apple; this is an orange; this is an acorn; this is an inkstand, etc.; this is a pen; this is a book, crayon, bell, etc.

Lead pupils to notice that sometimes *a* and sometimes *an* comes before the word that (names the object) tells what we are talking about. This fact is all that is wanted at this point. Then ask pupils to mention things with whose names they can use *an*, then those with whose names they can use *a*.

Give much practice until the ears of the children have become accustomed to notice the distinction. That it sounds better so is reason enough to give just now for using *a* or *an*.

The following words will be found convenient in teaching the use of *an*: (The words with which *a* is used can readily be collected by the teacher.) Acorn, angle, agate, aisle, alley, alligator, almanac, anchor, animal, ankle, ant, antelope, ape, apple, apron, arbor, ark, arm, armchair, arrow, aunt, awl, awning, axle, axe, eagle, ear, earring, eye, easel, edge, eel, egg, elbow, elephant, elm, eraser, emery, engine, envelope, elephant, express-wagon, errand, ice, ice-pitcher, ice-house, ice-chest, idol, image, inch, Indian, inkstand, iron, ivory, ivy, oak, oar, ocean, oilcloth, oil-can, office, omnibus, orange, orchard, organ, oven, owl, ox, oyster, overcoat, overshoe, onion, ostrich, umbrella, ulster, urn, uncle.

Conversational exercises which lead the children to use these words may be conducted in the following manner: Draw upon the board an express-wagon. (If a pupil bring into the room a toy express-wagon it will be better.) Question the pupils, requiring always full sentences in the answer.

What is this? What is it for? What are carried in an express-wagon?

What are the parts of an express-wagon?

What has an express-wagon?

What would you put into your express-wagon?

Give a lesson on the acorn and the oak in which the pupils shall be led to speak often of each.

ILLUSTRATION. Once there was a large, spreading tree whose leaves look like this: There were also a great many nuts on the tree. Some of the nuts fell off and a boy picked up many of them and carried them to his teacher. The nuts looked like this: What do you think those nuts were? Bring out the following answers: An acorn fell from the tree. I have an acorn in my right hand. An acorn grew on an oak tree? An acorn has a cup, etc., etc. An acorn is in the ledge. An acorn is upon the window-sill. We can roll an acorn. We can throw an acorn. We can plant an acorn.

## THE PLURAL.

To introduce the idea of the plural, the teacher says: Let me tell you a story. Once I saw, in a room where I was sitting, a little animal come out of a hole near the cupboard and run across the floor. It was about *so* long, and had a sharp nose, with whiskers on each side of its face; bright little eyes, that looked like little beads, in the sides of its head. It was covered with fur and had four legs, and a tail as long as *that*. What do you think it was?

*Pupils.* I think it was a mouse.

*T.* Yes; that is right. Pretty soon another little mouse ran out. Then how many were there?

*Pupils.* Then there were two.

*T.* Two what?

*P.* Two mice.

*T.* Say "Then there were two mice."

*P.* Then there were two mice.

*T.* What did you call that little animal that I told you about?

*P.* We called it a mouse.

*T.* What would you call two such animals?

*P.* We would call two such animals mice.

*T.* What would you call three such animals?

*P.* We would call three such animals mice.

*T.* What would you call one such animal?

*P.* We would call one such animal a mouse.

*T.* What would you call more than one such animal?

*P.* We would call more than one such animal mice.

*T.* Give me one word in your answer. What do you call one such animal?

*P.* A mouse.

*T.* More than one?

*P.* Mice.

*T.* What does a man have to draw him in a carriage?

*P.* He has a horse to draw him in a carriage.

*T.* Does he ever have more than one horse to draw him?

*P.* Yes; sometimes he has two horses.

*T.* Spell horse.

*P.* H-o-r-s-e.

*T.* Spell horses.

*P.* H-o-r-s-e-s.

*T.* How many animals does "horse" mean?

*P.* "Horse" means one animal.

*T.* How many animals does "horses" mean?

*P.* "Horses" means more than one animal.

When I came into school this morning a child came with me. Soon another child came in. Then who were in the room with me?

Then another came. Who were with me then? How many are one man and one man? One foot and one foot? One woman and one woman? One child and one child? One goose and one goose? One mouse and one mouse? One ox and one ox?

There were two children in a room and one of them went out. Who remained in the room?

Tell me something about one child. Say the same thing about more than one child.

Tell me something about one man. Say the same thing about more than one man.

I will say something about one and you may say the same about more than one: A mouse has bright eyes. An ox is not so swift as a horse. A good boy will be kind to his mother, etc.

Now I will say something about more than one and you may say the same about one: Rich men should help the poor.

What word means more than one child? Children means more than one child.

What word means more than one man? Men means more than one man, etc.

The word children means more than one what? The word men means more than one what? the word boys? the word foxes? the word churches? the word apples?

Continue such work several weeks and recur to it often.

Secure the plural form from the singular, the singular from the plural, and the use in a sentence of each form of the following words: —

Apple, arm, aunt, ball, barn, basket, bat, bear, bee, bell, bird, boat, book, boy, box, branch, brother, bug, bush, cage, cap, cart, cat, chain, cheek, chicken, child, clock, coat, crow, cup, day, desk, dog, doll, door, drum, duck, ear, egg, eye, face, fan, father, flower, foot, fork, fox, frog, game, girl, glass, goat, hand, hat, head, home, horn, horse, kid, kite, kitten, knife, lady, lamb, lamp, leaf, leg, man, mat, morning, mother, mouse, mouth, mug, name, nest, night, nose, nut, ox, pail, pan, paw, picture, plant, rabbit, rat, robin, rose, school, sheep, sister, slate, sled, spool, spoon, string, tail, teacher, tree, tub, uncle, wagon, wing.

Spend a few minutes daily on this work until the children are familiar with the plurals of these words. Say nothing about the formation of the plural.

## *Is* AND *Are*.

*Teacher.* Is this book new?
*Pupils.* Yes.
*T.* You are right; it is new. I wish you to tell me so.
*P.* The book is new.
*T.* Is this book new or old?
*P.* The book is old.
*T.* Tell me the same thing about these books.
*P.* The books are new.
The teacher places an apple upon the desk, and asks: Where is the apple?
*P.* The apple is on the desk.
*T.* (*putting down another apple*). Where are the apples?
*P.* The apples are on the desk.
*T.* (*taking up one of the apples, and pointing to the other*). Where is the apple?
*P.* The apple is on the desk.
*T.* (*putting down two or three apples*). Where are the apples?
Repeat the last two questions.
*T.* When do you say: The apple *is* on the desk?
*P.* We say "The apple is on the desk" when there is one apple.
*T.* When do you say: The apples *are* on the desk?
*T.* Where is the pointer?
*T.* Where are the pointers?
Extend, with many questions.

## *These* AND *Those* AS DEMONSTRATIVE PRONOUNS.

*Teacher.* What is this?
*Pupils.* That is a book.
*T.* What are these?
*P.* Those are books.
[If none of the pupils can give the correct answer after a minute's questioning, they must be told what answer to give.]
*T.* What are these?
*P.* Those are crayons.

*T.* What are these?
*P.* Those are acorns. Etc.

After many questions explain that you have called the objects *these* because they were near to you, while the children called them *those* because they were away from them.

Distribute objects to the children, giving two or three of a kind to each child. Of course there will not be objects enough for all. Some must listen until their turn comes. Let those who have objects tell what they are, showing first one object and then several. The child says: This is a flag. The class repeats: That is a flag. The child says: These are flags. The class repeats: Those are flags.

After the objects have been collected, ask the children: What word do we use for something near to us? *This.* [Full answer from the pupils.] For something away from us? *That.* For several things near to us? *These.* For several things away from us? *Those.*

## *This* AND *That*, *These* AND *Those*, AS PRONOMINAL ADJECTIVES.

Where is this slate? Where are these slates? [If the children say "the slate," ask "*what* slate" and they will reply "*that* slate."] Where does this box belong? Where do these boxes belong? What will this sphere do if I push it? [Plural.] What kind of surface has this sphere? [Plural.] How many faces has this cube? [Plural.]

Distribute objects to the children, several of the same kind to each child. Direct them to tell you something about one of the objects.

*Pupil.* This crayon is round.
*Class.* That crayon is round.
*P.* These crayons are round.
*C.* Those crayons are round. Etc., etc.

## *Is* AND *Are* AGAIN.

Let the pupil suit the action to the word and say: This is an eye; these are eyes; this is an ear; these are ears; this is a foot; these are feet; this is an apple; these are apples.

This might be made a pleasant concert exercise.

When such sentences are readily formed have the pupils repeat them again and emphasize the *is* or the *are;* as: This *is* an apple; these *are* apples. Etc.

The pupil will soon see that *is* is used when one thing is spoken about, and *are* when more than one is mentioned. Exercises in changing sentences so as to mean *one* or *more than one* should now be given; as: The bird is on its nest; the birds are on their nests. Hundreds of such sentences should be given by the pupils and changed in form as the teacher says *one, more than one.*

Putting something into a box in sight of the children, ask: What is in the box? The ring is in the box. Putting something else into the box, ask: What else is in the box? A pen is in the box.

*Teacher.* Put both answers together, and tell me what is in the box.
*Pupil.* A ring and a pen are in the box.
*T.* Of what is the pointer made?
*P.* The pointer is make of wood.
*T.* Of what is this cube made?
*P.* That cube is made of wood.
*T.* Of what are the pointer and the cube made?
*P.* The pointer and the cube are made of wood.
*T.* What is the shape of this ball?
*T.* What else is round?
*T.* Put both answers into one answer.
*P.* The ball and the marble are round.
*T.* Where is your overcoat?
*T.* Where is your hat?
*T.* Put both answers into one.

Use of **And.**

The teacher places two boys before the class, and says: What are the names of these boys?

*Ans.* Their names are James and John.

The teacher writes this on the board and has the class read it. She then places a third boy beside them and asks for their names.

The answer will probably be: Their names are James and John and Thomas.

This the teacher writes upon the board and has the class read it.

She then erases the first " and " in this sentence and has it read with but one "and." The class agree that this is better.

The teacher changes the order of the boys and asks again for their names, admonishing the pupils to be careful to put the " and " in the proper place. Four boys are named in the same way; three girls; five girls; then things in a chair; on a table; seen on the way to school; etc.

## Playing Store.

*Counter* — Seat of a chair.

*Stock* — Toys and little things children have brought from time to time.

*Storekeeper* — Some particularly exemplary boy.

*Customers* — Children who come, one at a time, to buy something which they afterward give as a present to some child in the room.

By this device complete sentences are secured. Also by increasing the number of articles bought a correct use of "and," and the condensation of statements are obtained; as, I would like to buy a doll, a fan, a flag, and an agate.

The verbs "buy" and "give" may be taught; also "has" and "have"; as: I have a book and a top; Robbie has a ball, a box, and a cup.

### *There is* AND *There are.*

*Teacher.* What is there on the table? Etc.

*Pupil.* There is a book on the table. There is a slate on the desk. There is a pencil in your hand. There is a picture on the blackboard. There is, etc.

*T.* John, what is there on your desk?

*John.* There is an apple on my desk.

*T.* Put another apple beside it and tell me again.

*J.* There are two apples on my desk.

[This answer may not be secured without an appeal to several pupils. When the right answer is obtained, emphasize it by commendation and repetition. Secure also the form: There are a ball and a cube on my desk.]

*T.* We shall want to use these words " there is " and " there are " often, and I will write them on the board, and we will make statements with them.

There is ———.
There are ———.

Now make me a statement beginning with "there is."

[A simple direction would be: Tell me something that is on the blackboard and begin by saying " there is."]

*P.* There is a picture of a bird on the blackboard. There is a vertical line on the blackboard. There is a piece of poetry to learn on the blackboard.

*T.* That is very well. Now Susan may tell me one other thing there is on the blackboard.

*Susan.* There is a picture of a house on the blackboard.

*T.* If I should make many pictures of houses on the board, then what would you tell me?

*S.* There are many pictures of houses on the blackboard.

*T.* Tell me two things that are on my table.

*P.* There are an inkstand and a Bible on your table.

*T.* Each of you think of something and tell me about it. Begin with " there is."

*P.* Various answers.

*T.* Each of you think of some things and tell me about them. Begin with "there are."

*P.* Various answers.

*T.* Each of you make a sentence beginning " there is " and then change it so that it will begin " there are."

*P.* Various answers.

## *Here* AND *There.*

*Teacher.* Think of something, point to it, and tell what is there.
*Pupil.* There is a window. Etc.
*T.* Think of something in this room, go and touch it, and tell us what is there.
*P.* Here is a register. Etc., etc.

This may be extended by the game of Hide and Go Seek. The teacher gives an object, as a top, to a child to hide. She shuts her eyes while the child is hiding the top, and all the children watch to see where it is hidden. As he is taking his seat the child calls " Ready." The teacher opens her eyes and says: " Where is the top?" calling the name of some child, who may either go and get it, and say: "Here is the top," or may point to the object, and say: " There it is," or " There is the top."

Thus the correct use of " where," " here," and "there" is obtained. By having first one and then more than one object of the same kind hidden a correct use of " is " and " are," " was " and " were " may be secured; as: Here is the ball; here are the balls; the ball was in the corner; the balls were behind the box.

By letting some child cover his eyes, as the teacher did, lead the children to use the interrogative form. The verbs " hide " and " find " may also be taught.

### Review Exercise.

Arrange small, bright-colored pictures upon a sheet of manilla paper or cardboard.

Send pupils to point out and name the objects; as: This is an apple; this is a box; these are birds; here are four spades; etc.

By having two such sheets, the pupil may be led to say: This is a drum; that is a horse; this is a cow; that is an ox; here are ——; and there are ——; on this sheet there are ——; on that sheet there are ——.

### *Has* AND *Have.*

(*Put a pencil on Mary's desk.*) Who has a pencil on her desk?
(*Put a pencil on John's desk.*) What has John on his desk?
Tell me what they both have on their desks.
What has Carrie in the dressing-room?
What has Emma in the dressing-room?
Tell me what Carrie and Emma have in the dressing-room.
Tell me what John and James have in the dressing-room.
What parts has a chair?
What parts have chairs?
What I tell you about several things you may tell me about one thing.

*Teacher.* Elephants have big trunks, big ears, and small eyes.

*Pupil.* An elephant has a big trunk, big ears, and small eyes.
*T.* Houses have chimneys, doors, and windows.
*P.* A house has chimneys, doors, and windows.
*T.* A cat has bright eyes and sharp claws. Tell me the same about more than one cat.
*P.* Cats have, etc.

Continue the exercise, saying to the pupils *one* and *more than one*, until they readily change the singular to the plural, and the plural to the singular, using the verbs "is" and "are," "has" and "have."

## *Was* and *Were.*

*Teacher.* Mary, were you at school yesterday?
*Mary.* Yes; I was here.
*T.* Who else was here yesterday?
*M.* Alice was here.
*T.* Tell me that about both of you.
*M.* Alice and I were at school yesterday.
*T.* Tell me two more who were here.
*M.* Harry and Walter were here.
*T.* If you wanted to tell me that you are at school to-day, what would you say?
*M.* I am at school to-day.
*T.* If you wanted to tell me that you were at school yesterday, what would you say?
*M.* I was at school yesterday.
*T.* If you say "I am," do you mean *now?*
*M.* Yes; "I am" means now.
*T.* If you say "I was," do you mean now?
*M.* No; "I was" means before now.
*T.* Tell me something that happened yesterday.

The teacher writes these sentences on the board and directs the pupils to read the sentences, inserting "is" or "are," "was" or "were" in the blank spaces.

The book —— new.
The hat —— old.
The birds —— flying.

The pictures —— pretty.
Sam —— here yesterday.
Emma —— at my house last week.
Tom —— late twice a few days ago.
—— the sentences written as well yesterday as they —— to-day?
—— you there this morning?
—— John with you?
Where —— you when I called?
Who —— that man with you?
Who —— those men with you?
You —— late this morning.
They —— going home yesterday.

Carrie, ask Maggie where she was before school. Ask her what she was doing at noon. Ask her if she was at home last evening.

Thomas, ask me if I was here early.

[The pupil will probably begin, "Was you —— "]

### FORMING WORDS INTO SENTENCES.

The teacher may write sentences upon suitable slips of stiff paper, and then cut the words apart and put them into an envelope. Giving each pupil such an envelope, let him form the words into the sentence upon his desk. If far enough advanced, he may then copy the sentence upon his slate.

Then each word may be used in a new sentence; or two words only of the list may be given in each sentence, etc.

### USE OF ADJECTIVES.

(a) Give to the children objects with some quality so prominent as not to be overlooked: an old book; a new book; a hard ball; a soft ball; a long pencil; a short pencil; a large cube; a small cube; a sharp pencil; a dull pencil.

Then ask them: What have you? What kind of —— have you? Who else has a ——? Is yours a —— ——? What kind of —— is yours?

This lesson may be given with objects distributed, afterwards with objects shown.

(b) Give or show the children objects with a decided quality, and obtain from them the word expressing the opposite quality.

Begin with the objects used in (a) and proceed to others: a crooked line; a bright tin; a sweet apple; a good drawing; a sharp knife; a tall man. What is this? What kind of —— is it? If it were not a —— ——, what kind of —— would it be?

Think of an apple. What kind of apple did you think of? Who thought of a different kind? Who can now think of still another kind of apple?

Continue in this way with many objects.

*Teacher.* What kind of boy is John?
*Pupil* John is a good boy. John is a little boy.
*T.* What kind of book have you?
*P.* I have a new book. I have a clean book. I have a torn book.
*T.* What kind of pencil have you?
*P.* I have a slate pencil.
*T.* Can you tell me anything about it?
*P.* It is sharp and will make a mark.
*T.* What can you tell me about this slate?
*P.* That slate is new. That slate is clean. That slate is black.
*T.* Can you tell me all that about the slate and say "that slate" but once?
*P.* That slate is new, clean, and black.
*T.* Tell me two things about this flag.
*P.* That flag is small and new.
*T.* With what do we sharpen pencils? With what sort of knife do we do it? If a knife is not sharp, what sort of knife is it? How may a knife be? How may pencils be? How may water be? How may a boy be? How may the weather be? How may a lesson be?

## Description.

Occasionally request each pupil to bring something to school in the afternoon, to show and tell something about.

Result. — This is my doll. I call her Kitty. I love to play with my doll.

This is my knife. It has a handle and two blades. I use it to cut sticks with.

# FIRST YEAR.

This box is made of wood. It has a top, put on with hinges, and a clasp to keep it shut. My Uncle James gave it to me. I use it to keep my playthings in.

This exercise might occur for a few minutes each day until need of variety was felt. It could then be laid aside for a time and afterwards be resumed as an occasional exercise.

## THE PRONOUN.

Introduce the pronoun thus: —

*Teacher.* Mary, you may hold up your book so that the school can see it. What is she doing?

*Pupil.* She is holding up her book.

*T.* Who is holding up her book?

*P.* Mary.

*T.* Tell me that in a full sentence.

*P.* Mary is holding up her book.

*T.* What is Mary doing?

*P.* She is holding up her book.

*T.* Whom do you mean by *she?*

*P.* I mean Mary by *she.*

*T.* Then what word will *she* stand for?

*P.* *She* will stand for Mary.

*T.* Could it stand for any other word?

*P.* *She* could stand for any girl's name.

*T.* Would *he* stand for any girl's name?

*P.* No. *He* would stand for a boy's name.

*T.* Would *she* stand for a woman's name? Would *he* stand for a man's name?

## THE PERSONAL PRONOUNS.

1. A pupil may be asked as he holds up his object to tell you what he has, saying, I have a cup; and with successive objects, as before: I have an agate. I have a toothpick. I have a splint. I have a cube. I have a sphere.

2. The teacher may hold up objects and secure the statements: You have a bean. You have a pin. You have a pear. You have an orange. You have an inkstand. You have a pen.

3. Children in different parts of the room may hold up objects to be named, and a pupil may tell them: You have a slate, etc.

4. The teacher may change the form of the exercise at this point, and as the children exhibit their various objects may say, "Instead of telling *Mary* what she has, you may tell *me* what she has." The answer secured will be: Mary has a doll. John has a knife. Peter has a top.

5. *Teacher.* Can you not tell me what Peter has without saying *Peter?* Can you use some other word than *Peter* to tell me that Peter has a top?

*Pupil.* He has a top.

*T.* What else has Peter?

*P.* He has a kite. He has a pointer. He has a box, etc.

[Let Peter show these things to bring out the statement given.]

6. *T.* What did you tell me Mary has?

*P.* Mary has a doll.

*T.* Do not say *Mary.* Use some other word in place of Mary as you did when you told me what Peter had.

*P.* She has a doll.

Let Mary now show other objects, and secure several such statements. Let Susan and Jane and Thomas and John successively exhibit objects until *he* and *she* are readily used.

7. Two pupils may come together to the platform and, holding one object, may say: We have a pointer. We have a flag. We have an eraser. We have a hat, etc.

8. As these pupils hold up the successive objects, the teacher may ask the school to tell them what they have, and secure the statements: You have a basin. You have a basket. You have a stick, etc.

9. *T.* Instead of telling *them* what they have, you may tell *me* what they have.

*P.* They have a basin. They have a basket. They have a globe. They have a cap, etc.

## PREDICATION OF ACTION.

*Teacher.* What can a dog do?

*Pupil.* A dog can run.

*T.* What else can run?
*P.* A cat can run. A —— can run, etc.
*T.* What can fly?
*P.* A bird can fly, etc.
*T.* What can a fish do? What can a boy do? What can a hen do? What can a lion do? What can a monkey do? Etc.
*T.* What can boys do?
*P.* Boys can run. Boys can play ball. Boys can row boats, etc.
*T.* What can a man do?
*P.* A man can drive a horse. A man can keep a store. A man can build a house.

### Description of Actions.

To describe acts is a valuable exercise.

By appropriate means it will be easy to secure such sentences as these: You opened the door. You put a book upon the table. You looked at the thermometer. You walked slowly across the floor. You walked rapidly across the floor. You wrote upon the board.

A pupil may be given a whispered direction and the class may tell from the deed what was said to the pupil: as, You told James to give John his book. The teacher told James to carry a book to John. Miss Brown told James to let John have a book.

### Day-dreaming.

*Teacher.* You may put your heads down upon the desk, close your eyes, and dream of what you can see at home.

Wake up, now, and tell us your dreams. Richard, what did you see in your dream?

Richard relates his dream, and others are called upon to do the same.

The children may be directed to dream about a boat ride, a picnic, a school in another town, etc., etc.

This exercise gives freedom of expression and develops individuality and originality of thought.

In such exercises, rarely notice any incorrect forms of speech, as fear of criticism is sure to clip the wings of the child's imagination.

# CHAPTER II.—SECOND YEAR.

The work for the pupil now becomes more extended and much of it is written.

The order in which the following topics are presented may be varied by the teacher, though the natural order of sequence of many of the topics is that given here.

For early written work card sentences are convenient. [See p. 31.]
A variety of sentences may be formed with the same words.
The original sentence may have been: —
The teacher loves a boy who is always polite and kind.

With these words the pupil may make the following sentences, one at a time, and copy them on his slate: —
The polite boy loves a kind teacher.
The kind boy always loves a polite teacher.
The teacher who is always kind loves a polite boy.
The boy is always kind.
The teacher is always polite.
The boy who loves a kind teacher is always polite.

By putting into the envelope an extra noun and verb, a much greater variety of sentences may be formed.

## QUESTION AND ANSWER.

To answer the precise question asked, and not some similar question, is usual only with cultivated people.

The habit of giving such answers, next to the habit of speaking in full sentences, is the one most fundamental and important in language training, as usually conducted in schools.

ILLUSTRATION. "Whose hat is that?" "That is Reuben's hat." Not, "That hat belongs to Reuben." "What do you see on the blackboard?" "I see a picture upon the blackboard." Not, "There is a picture upon the blackboard."

From the first and always, insist upon the answer's following the form of the question.

### To use the Personal Pronouns as Subjects, also Nouns and Pronouns in the Same Sentence.

*Teacher.* Mary, show me your book. What have you?
*Mary.* I have a book.
*T.* John, show me your book. What have you?
*J.* I have a book.
*T.* John, tell me what you and Mary have.
*J.* We have books.
*T.* Use Mary's name and tell me again what you have.
*J.* Mary and I have books.
*T.* Frank, show me your book. What have you?
*Frank.* I have a book.
*T.* Frank, tell me what you and Mary and John have.
*F.* We have books.
*T.* Use their names and tell me.
*F.* Mary and John and I have books.
*T.* Tell me again and leave out the first *and*.
*F.* Mary, John, and I have books.
*T.* Use words for Mary and John that are not their names.
[Tell me that without using their names.]
*F.* She, he, and I have books.
[If you have difficulty in securing this answer, you may aid the pupils by copying upon the blackboard the previous answer, *Mary, John, and I have books*, and then securing the word *she* in place of Mary and *he* in place of John.]
*T.* Mary, what have I?
*Mary.* You have a book.
*T.* What have we?
*M.* We have books.
*T.* Speak about us separately.
*M.* You and I have books.

*T.* Frank, you may hold up your book. Now, Mary, tell us about yourself, Frank, and me.

*M.* You and Frank and I have books.

*T.* Leave out one of the *ands.* Which one?

*M.* The first.

*T.* Yes. How then will it be?

*M.* You, Frank, and I have books.

*T.* John and Edward may stand.

John, what are you doing?

Edward, what are you doing?

John, what is Edward doing?

Edward, what is John doing?

John, what are you and Edward doing?

[We are standing.]

Answer with one word for you and one for Edward.

*John.* He and I are standing.

*T.* Edward, what are you and I doing?

*T.* Answer with one word for us both.

*T.* Answer with one word for each of us.

Direct two girls to look out of the window, and then question them similarly. Question the class about these girls.

Join the girls and secure the use of "You, she, and I," "You, Mary, and I," "You, Emma, and Mary," etc.

*Teacher.* Who is coming to school this afternoon?

*Pupil.* I am coming.

*T.* Who else is coming?

*P.* Mary is coming.

*T.* Tell me that you and Mary are coming to school this afternoon.

*P.* Mary and I are coming to school this afternoon.

*T.* Am I coming?

*P.* Yes, you are coming.

*T.* Now tell me about you, Mary, and me.

*P.* You, Mary, and I are coming.

By questioning secure the use of the following sentences: —

John and I can see the bird.

He and I will go for you.

# SECOND YEAR. 39

You, he, and I will study.
You were here yesterday.
[Such sentences should be repeated many times to prevent the error *you was.*]

## POSSESSIVE OF PERSONAL PRONOUNS.

*Teacher.* Mary, is that your book?
*Mary.* Yes.
*T.* Say so.
*M.* This is my book.
*T.* Whose book is this?
*M.* That is your book.
*T.* You may take it and then tell me whose book it is.
*M.* This is your book.
*T.* Whose book is this?
*M.* That is Ray's book.
*T.* If Ray had it, what would he say about it?
*M.* He would say, "It is my book."
*T.* What do you say about it?
*M.* It is his book. It is Ray's book.

By a similar method, secure: —
　　It is our ——.
　　It is their ——.
　　It is her ——. Etc.
Also —
　　That is his ——.
　　That is our ——.
　　These are our ——.
　　Those are her ——. Etc.

## OBJECTIVE FORMS OF PERSONAL PRONOUNS.

*Teacher.* Samuel, you may give Peter something. What did you give Peter?
*Samuel.* I gave him a marble.
*T.* What word in your answer stands for Peter?
*S.* *Him* stands for Peter.

*T.* Use the word *him* in another sentence, and tell me for whom it stands. [Several answers.]

*T.* If you put the word *her* in place of *him* in the sentences you have given, what difference in meaning would it make?

*T.* John, you may bring me your book. What did I tell you to do?

*John.* You told me to bring you my book.

*T.* Tell Mary what I told you.

*J.* The teacher told me to bring her my book.

*T.* Mary, you may bring me your book. What have I told you to do?

*Mary.* You told me to bring you my book.

*T.* What did I tell you and John to do?

*M.* You told John and me to bring you our books.

*T.* Make three sentences, each having the word *us* in it; *you; them; me; him; her.*

NOTE.—This is a difficult construction and should have much practice. The every-day errors will give the teacher abundant examples for corrections.

## OBJECTIVE CASE OF PRONOUNS. — *Continued.*

*Teacher.* (Give book to boy.) What did I do?

*Pupil.* You gave me a book.

*T.* To whom did I give a book?

(Ask another pupil the same question.)

*P.* You gave a book to John.

*T.* Use a word not his name to stand for John.

*P.* You gave a book to him.

*T.* (Giving a book to a girl, ask another pupil:) What am I doing now?

*P.* You are giving a book to Alice.

*T.* Answer the question, using no name.

*P.* You are giving a book to her.

*T.* Did I give a book to you?

Did I give a book to John?

Did I give a book to Alice?

Did I give books to John and Alice?

Ask John if I gave him a book.

John, you may write your name on the board. Eddie, you may do the same. John, what did I tell you to do? Whom else did I tell to do the same thing?

Answer both my questions in one sentence.

Eddie, what did I tell you and John to do?

Use one word that stands for a name in your answer.

*P.* You told John and me to write our names, etc.

*T.* Use two words that stand for names in your answer.

*P.* You told him and me, etc.

*T.* Use one word that stands for both your names in your answer.

*P.* You told us to write, etc.

*T.* Henry, what did I tell John and Eddie to do?

*T.* Use their names in the answer. Use a word in place of their names.

Henry, you may go into the hall and come back. Henry, whom did I send into the hall?

Mary may go into the hall and return. Did I send Mary into the hall?

Whom did I send, Henry? (Use two pronouns.)

Whom did I send, Mary? (Use two pronouns.)

John, whom did I send? (Use two pronouns.)

Carrie, whom did I send? (Use one pronoun.)

Henry, ask Mary whom I sent.

Thomas, did I send you into the hall?

Thomas, did I send you and James into the hall?

Use a name and a word for a name in your answer.

Use two words for names in your answer.

Use one word for names in your answer.

## The Possessive of Nouns.

[See Dictation Exercises, p. 52.]

*Teacher.* John, whose book have you?

*John.* I have Mary's book.

*T.* Whose slate have you?

*J.* I have Peter's slate.

*T.* Let me write what you said on the board, and you may read it to me.

*J.* I have Mary's book. I have Peter's slate.

*T.* Do you notice how I wrote *Mary's* and *Peter's?* Let me show you how to spell *Mary's.* We call the little mark before the *s,* an apostrophe, and we spell *Mary's* capital M-a-r-y-apostrophe-s. You may spell *Mary's.*

*J.* Capital M-a-r-y-apostrophe-s.

*T.* Spell *Peter's.*

*J.* Capital P-e-t-e-r-apostrophe-s.

*T.* When you see apostrophe-s at the end of a word, you may know that something belongs to the one whose name has the apostrophe-s after it. What does this sentence on the board tell you belongs to Mary?

*J.* It tells me that a book belongs to Mary.

*T.* What does *this* sentence tell you belongs to Peter?

*J.* It tells me that the slate I have belongs to Peter.

*T.* Susan, you may show the class something that belongs to you. Walter, whose doll is that?

*Walter.* That is Susan's doll.

*T.* Tell me how to write *Susan's* on the board.

*W.* Capital S-u-s-a-n-apostrophe-s.

*T.* You may all write on your slates a sentence that has the word *Henry's* in it.

### Review Exercises.

Illustrating his statements with an undressed doll, each pupil may give a little lecture from the platform, upon anatomy.

This is Lottie's doll. It has a head (pointing to it), a body, two arms, and two legs. The parts of the head are the skull and face, etc., etc. This exercise should be extended until all the pupils know and can readily tell all of anatomy that the teacher desires them to understand at this stage of school life.

The same thing can be done with leaves, plants, and fruits, with animals and pictures of animals, with the plane and solid geometrical figures or models used in the lessons in drawing.

## Use of *Not*.

*Teacher.* John may come to the platform and stand where all can see him. Has he his hat on?
*Pupils.* No.
*T.* Say so.
*P.* John has not his hat on. John does not have on his hat.
*T.* Has he a ball in his hand?
*P.* No; he does not have a ball in his hand.
*T.* Let Albert stand beside him. Have they their hats on?
*P.* No; they do not have on their hats.
*T.* Do you think they would wear their hats in school?
*P.* I don't think they would.

Give further drills on the use of the negative by having the pupils change statements to negations.

Do this by writing several statements upon the blackboard and asking the children to copy them and make the sentences mean the opposite by inserting *not*.

## How to Use *A* and *An*.

Put words having *a* before them in a column on the blackboard, and others having *an* before them in another column. One column will have names beginning with consonants, the other will have names beginning with vowels. Let the pupils notice that there is an *a* column and an *an* column. Call the attention of the class to the second column. What is the first name word? Apple. What is the first letter of this word? Is there any other word in this column that begins with *a*? Yes; arm. Is there any word in the first column that begins with *e*? The pupil readily finds that all the words in the second column begin with *a, e, i, o,* or *u*, and that none of the words of the first column begins with these letters.

He now tries other words, and finds that all words having *an* before them begin with one of these letters, and *says so*.

The statements now easily secured from the pupil will be sufficient rules for the use of *a* and *an*.

For further drill the teacher may write lists of words upon the blackboard, and require the pupils to read them with *a* or *an* before them and to copy them with *a* or *an* before them.

The pupils may be still further trained to the correct use of *a* and *an* by having them use these words in their work in physiology, saying, "I have an eye, I have an ear, I have a nose," etc.

Pupils may be asked to name as many objects as they can before whose names *a* is used; before whose names *an* is used.

## ADVERBS.

*Teacher.* How do I wish you to come to the class?

*Pupils.* You wish us to come quietly. You wish us to come quickly. You wish us to come pleasantly. You wish us to come with our slates clean and pencils ready.

*T.* Very good. Those words that tell *how* we do things we will call *how-words*. By and by I will give you another name for them, but now that will be easy for you to remember. Tell me *how* you walk.

*P.* We walk slowly. We walk quietly. We walk fast.

*T.* How do you write on your slates, and what kind of writing do you make?

*P.* We write nicely on our slates, and then we have nice writing.

By similar questioning obtain:—

When we are careful we write carefully.

A kind child will speak kindly to all.

*T.* Put a *how*-word into these sentences:—

A rapid writer is one who writes ———.

A safe horse carries you ———.

I know that the boy is cross, because he speaks ———.

It must be a careless lad who has done his work so ———.

When we are gay we act ———.

That was loud reading, for we were reading ———.

A modest child will speak ———.

That was ——— done by an awkward boy.

The girl was sad, and walked ——— homeward.

Their merry laughter rings ——— out.

*T.* How does James do his work? Carefully, etc.

## SECOND YEAR.

### IRREGULAR VERBS. —*Write*.

*Teacher.* What do you do on your slates?
*Pupils.* We write upon our slates.
*T.* Spell *write*.
*P.* W-r-i-t-e, write.
*T.* Write this word *write* upon your slates, and Tommy may write it on the blackboard. Did you ever write upon your slates before?
*P.* Yes; we wrote upon our slates yesterday.
*T.* How do you spell *wrote?*
*P.* W-r-o-t-e, wrote.
*T.* Write the word *wrote* also on your slates and on the blackboard under the other word which I told you to write. Write your names at the top of your slates. What have you done?
*P.* We have written our names upon our slates.
*T.* Spell *written*.
*P.* W-r-i-t-t-e-n, written.
*T.* Write the word *written* under the other words. What words have you on your slates?
*P.* Write, wrote, written.
*T.* Put the word *write* into a sentence. Put the word *wrote* into a sentence. Put the word *written* into a sentence. Put *write, wrote,* or *written* into these sentences where I have left the blanks.

I —— on my slate every day.
Laura —— on her slate yesterday.
Edna —— in her book yesterday.
Ella has —— her name on her slate.
Tommy may —— his name on the blackboard.
I have —— a letter this morning.
The letter was —— in Boston.
Last night we —— letters to our friends.
Next week we shall —— again.
I found the letter had been badly ——.
One boy has —— very carelessly.
To-morrow I hope he will —— better. Etc.

*Teacher.* What are the three forms of *write* that we have learned?
*P.* Write, wrote, written.

*T.* There are two more forms that I wish you to learn. You may write on your slates this: write, ———, wrote, written, ———. What have you been doing?

*P.* We have been writing.

*T.* Spell *writing.*

*P.* W-r-i-t-i-n-g, writing.

*T.* That is the new form I wish you to learn. You may put it at the end of the line with the others. Should I say, Tommy writes on his slate, or Tommy write on his slate?

*P.* Tommy *writes* on his slate.

*T.* Spell *writes.*

*P.* W-r-i-t-e-s, writes.

*T.* You may put *writes* after the *write* in the line which you have written on your slates. What have you now on your slates?

*P.* Write, writes, wrote, written, writing.

*T.* These are the five forms of *write*. Say them to me.

Pupils repeat.

*T.* Copy them on your slates again. Make sentences and put one of these words, *is, are, was, were, will, may, can, next week, to-morrow, this morning, yesterday, last term, has, have, had, shall be, must,* into each sentence with some form of the verb *write.*

NOTE.— The teacher can assign a part of these words for a lesson, and may use other auxiliaries and time-words to secure variety and practice.

Put upon the blackboard, to remain as long as useful: —

### Know.

| | |
|---|---|
| to-day | had |
| yesterday | may |
| this morning | can |
| to-morrow | may have |
| next week | can have |
| is | might |
| are | could |
| was | might have |
| were | could have |

| | |
|---|---|
| has | shall be |
| have | will be |
| shall | shall have been |
| will | will have been |
| shall have | could have been |
| will have | might have been |

Give the direction: Use in a sentence some form of *know* with each of the words below the bar. This will be good seat work. At first, not so many time-words and auxiliaries should be put upon the board as are here given. Pupils should be encouraged to make long and interesting sentences.

### *Take.*

*Teacher (writing the word "take" upon the blackboard).* Who can give me a sentence that contains this word?

*Pupil.* The scholars *take* their books home every night.

*T.* John, you may write that sentence on the board, and the rest may copy it upon your slates. If you said the same thing about *Mary* that you have just said about *the scholars*, what would your sentence be?

*P.* Mary *takes* her books home every night.

*T.* Write that sentence also. What did Mary do with her books last night?

*P.* She *took* them home.

*T.* Write that too, John. Has she ever done this before?

*P.* Yes, she has *taken* them home many nights.

*T.* Put that sentence down under the others. If you were to meet her with her books after school and ask her what she was doing with them, what do you think she would say?

*P.* I am *taking* my books home.

*T.* Let us have that sentence placed with the rest. What are the sentences which you have written?

*P.* The scholars take their books home every night, etc.

Two or three other irregular verbs may be treated in the same manner.

At length it will be sufficient for the teacher to write the forms of an irregular verb on the blackboard, as, *see, sees, saw, seen, seeing,* and say to the pupils: Use each of these forms in two sentences.

To learn the irregular verbs so as to use them properly is a large task, and will require patient drilling month after month and year after year. But little folks like such work, and while learning these forms are learning many things besides.

### Dictation Exercise.

Write and fill the blanks: —

Henry's father is a blacksmith. He —— a great many horses. Last Wednesday he —— ten. He has —— several already this morning, and is —— one now.

It was very cold last night. The water —— in our kitchen. If it —— much harder, the pipes will burst. Do you think it will —— again to-night? When the river is —— over, all can skate. Do you think it is —— now?

Such work should be extended at the discretion of the teacher.

### Irregular Verbs. — Reviews.

For a review exercise in irregular verbs the following and similar sentences may be written upon the board and the pupils may copy them and write the answer in the form here given: —

Did you come to school this morning?
Yes, I came to school this morning.
Did you find the ball?
Did John break his pen?
Did Mary catch the train?
Did the water freeze last night?
Did you forget to tell your mother?
Did Peter forgive John?
Did he bring his book with him?
Did she sing sweetly?
Did the baby drink his milk?

Suggestive questions beginning with *Did,* to cause the pupils to use the past tense of irregular verbs can be varied by beginning them

with some interrogative word; as, *When did* your father give you that?
*Why did* the colt break his halter?
*Where* did you find the ball?
*Whose* slate did you break?
*How* did you come to school?
At what time did ——? Etc.

After pupils have become familiar with this exercise it may be reversed, and pupils may be required to ask questions beginning with *Did*, for which the following are answers: —

Yes, he hung up his cap.
Yes, they flung down their bats.
Yes, Margaret swept the room.
Yes, Thomas wrote the letter.

Next, the verb in its present form may be given on the board, and pupils may be required to write both questions and answers in the forms indicated.

The pupils may next be required to put their answers into the form, "Yes, —— have (has) just now —— "; as, —

Did you find your book?
Yes, I have just found it.
Did Susan tell you the story?
Yes, she has just told it to me.

For a further exercise, require both question and answer to be prepared by the pupils from the list of present forms upon the board.

The two forms of answers may be required. This will introduce in question and answer the three principal parts of each verb assigned.

Keep a list of irregular verbs at first with, and afterwards without, their principal parts, upon the board for frequent oral and written drill.

The following is a suitable list of irregular verbs to be taught during the second year: break, bring, buy, catch, come, draw, drive, eat, fall, find, fly, freeze, give, go, grow, hide, lay, lie, read, run, see, take, tell, throw, write.

## Adjectives. — Comparative Degree.

*Teacher.* Mary, you may draw a horizontal line on the board and write your name beside it. John may draw another horizontal line near Mary's and write his name beside his line. Children, can you see any difference between these lines?

*Pupil.* One is longer than the other. One is heavier than the other. One is straighter than the other.

*T.* What is the difference between Mary's line and John's line?

*P.* Mary's line is lighter than John's.

*T.* Tell me something that will mean the same, but begin your statement with *John's line is* ——.

*P.* John's line is heavier than Mary's.

*T.* What other difference is there?

*P.* Mary's line is longer than John's.

*T.* You have told me something about Mary's line. Tell me something about John's line.

*P.* John's line is shorter than Mary's.

*T.* Which line is the shorter line?

*P.* John's line is the shorter line.

*T.* Which line is the straighter line?

*P.* Mary's line is the straighter line.

*T.* Which line did Mary draw?

*P.* Mary drew the longer line. Mary drew the straighter line. Mary drew the lighter line. Mary drew the upper line.

Have pupils compare two knives, two apples, two books, two sticks, two pictures, two toys, two boys, two girls, two houses, two horses, two specimens of writing on the board, etc., until the comparative degree can be used freely in all forms of sentences.

Do not introduce more than two objects at a time for comparison, nor give any occasion for the use of the superlative degree for two or three months after the introduction of the comparison of objects by means of adjectives.

The erroneous use of the superlative degree for the comparative may be largely prevented by this precaution.

## A Further Exercise with Adjectives.

Have two pencils, sticks, or books conspicuously different in some respect.

*Teacher.* What kind of pencil is this?
*Pupil.* That is a long pencil.
*T.* In which hand is it?
*P.* It is in your right hand.
Show another pencil in the left hand.
*T.* What kind of pencil is this?
*P.* That is a short pencil.
*T.* Which pencil is this?
*P.* That is the long pencil.
*T.* Tell the difference between the pencil in my left hand and the one in my right hand; between the pencil in my right hand and the one in my left hand? Which of the two pencils is this?
*P.* That is the shorter of the two pencils.
*T.* Which of the two pencils is this?

So with other things. Secure the words *larger, smaller, thicker, thinner, wider, narrower.*

Have two children stand.
*T.* Are these children of the same height?
*T.* Is John taller or shorter than William?
*T.* Compare William's height with John's height.
*T.* Compare William's weight with John's weight.
*T.* Compare William's age with John's age.
Reverse these questions.

Present two pieces of paper or cloth of the same color, but of different shades, and ask the children to compare them.

Direct pupils to copy from the board the following sentences, and fill each blank with one of these words: sly, clean, little, tin, old, red.

1. This is a —— apple.
2. The —— box has a thimble in it.
3. The —— hen clucks to her —— chickens.
4. You should keep your books ——.
5. See the —— fox run at the hen.

## BLACKBOARD COMPOSITION.

[Have on the blackboard a list of words promiscuously arranged which are familiar to the pupils and suitable for the exercise.]

The teacher has the class read sentences in concert as she points out the words, and then has some one repeat the sentences. A careful preparation on the teacher's part will be necessary to give interest to this work.

When the class reads well and can readily repeat the sentences, let a pupil take the pointer and be the leader of the class in sentences of his own invention. If he asks for some additional word, write it for him.

He should not begin pointing until the sentence is fully formed in his own mind.

The teacher may say, "Make me a sentence beginning with *shall, we, John,* etc., or containing *top, me, is, are, was, were,* etc."

Pupils at their seats may print such sentences with their letter boxes.

At first just words enough for the sentence may be given; as, *pig, the, run, see, fat; the, milk, old, gives, cow.*

Then combine the words of the two sentences; as, *the, the, fat, milk, pig, old, cow, see, gives, run.*

Then extend.

## COMBINING STATEMENTS.

The tendency of children, and of persons of childish attainments, is to speak in short, simple sentences and to unite these in a series of statements by the use of *and*.

This is a serious defect in speech, though scarcely noticed by many teachers, because it does not involve the violation of any rules of grammar. Such sentences are correct grammatically, but awkward rhetorically.

The defect is one of failure to grasp several things at one time. The mind moves successively from one small thought to another with little comprehension of the relations of these thoughts.

The child who says, "I see James. He is on the platform. He is standing by a chair," is quite inferior in power of expression, and probably in mental grasp, to the one who says, "I see James standing by a chair on the platform."

When a series of statements like those given above is received, it should be accepted only as preparatory to something better, and the child should be required to put his statements together into one statement, being assisted, if need be, in getting the best form.

### Dictation Exercises for Second Year.

[See notes on dictation work, p. 5.]

(Teach that a statement begins with a capital and is followed by a period. The word *statement* will need no explanation if it is used frequently, as it should be, in all conversations between teacher and pupil. Before giving a dictation, teach from the blackboard any words that the pupils are likely to misspell, or not to understand.)

I. The birds come in the spring. They build their nests in the trees. Early in the morning they sing sweetly. In the autumn they go away to warmer countries. Some birds stay here all winter.

II. A sphere has a curved surface. A cube has a plane surface. The surface of the cylinder is both curved and plane. The sphere has but one face. The cube has six faces. The cylinder has three faces.

III. (Teach that a question is followed by ?. Call it "a question mark.")
1. Do you hear the birds sing?
2. Did you come to school early?
3. Will you please pass me the cylinder?
4. Do you like to skate?
5. What do you like to do in summer?

IV. 1. At what time did you come to school this morning? I came at a quarter before nine.
2. How many pencils did you bring to me? I brought you four pencils.
3. What did you see in the street this morning? I saw a horse running away.

V. (Teach that the word *I* is always a capital.)
1. My friend and I went yesterday to see the animals at the park.
2. How old do you think that I am?
3. When I come this afternoon I will bring you a pretty picture.
4. May I use your pencil?
5. Shall I help you move that table?

VI. (Teach that persons' names begin with capital letters.)
1. John has a little sister named Jessie.
2. Yesterday I saw Henry walking with his cousin George.
3. Do you think that Lucy is taller than I am?
4. Will you tell Mary that I would like to speak with her?
5. Shall I pass this book to Carrie?
6. May I speak to Albert?

VII. 1. John is a kind little boy.
2. I saw Herbert politely assisting a lame girl to cross the street.
3. Would you not be pleased to see Willie?
4. When did you hear from Charlie and Sammie?
5. Helen and Louisa are busy little girls.

VIII. (Teach how to write a full name, initials and surname, etc.)
1. Write your own full name.
2. Write your initials.
3. Write the initials of your given names and your whole surname.
4. Write these names: Henry W. Longfellow, John G. Whittier, Ralph Waldo Emerson, James Russell Lowell, William Cullen Bryant.

IX. (Teach that names of places begin with capitals. If the name consists of more than one word, each word will begin with a capital.)
1. We live in the United States.
2. The United States is a part of North America.
3. New York is the largest city in the United States.
4. Boston and Providence are cities in New England.
5. Philadelphia and Chicago are large cities.

X. (Teach use of caret, and hyphen at end of line.)
1. London is a very large city in England.

2. France and Germany are important countries in Europe.
3. Paris is the largest city in France.
4. Berlin is the largest city in Germany.

XI. (Teach that the names of the days of the week begin with capitals.)
1. Last Monday I went down the river with Annie and Hattie.
2. John and Eddie hope to go skating next Saturday.
3. Did you go to church last Sunday?
4. Shall you take your music lesson Wednesday or Thursday?

XII. 1. May I come to your house next Tuesday?
2. Helen is coming from New York next Friday.
3. I expect several friends to visit me next Wednesday.
4. The steamship sails for France on Friday.
5. Will you go to Boston with me on Thursday?

XIII. (Teach that the names of the months begin with capitals.)
1. Christmas comes in December.
2. Thanksgiving comes in November.
3. January is a cold month.
4. July and August are very warm months.
5. I like May and June the best.
6. February is the shortest month.

XIV. 1. In March and November the wind blows hard.
2. In April it often rains.
3. April showers bring May flowers.
4. Some fruits ripen in September.
5. The leaves begin to fall in October.

XV. (Teach the use of apostrophe and *s* to show possession, to show *whose* something is.)
1. Have you seen John's slate this morning?
2. Last Sunday Henry's little sister went to church for the first time.
3. Mary's cloak and hat are new.
4. The teacher praised Charlie's writing.

5. Last Wednesday George's dog was lost.
6. Next summer we are all going to visit Lucy's friends in Pomfret.

XVI. (Teach how to write Mr., Mrs., Miss, and Dr.)
1. Write your father's name. Write what people call him when they speak to him. (Mr. Green.)
2. Write your mother's name.
3. Write your teacher's name.
4. Write some man's name.
5. Write some lady's name beginning with Mrs.
6. Write some lady's name beginning with Miss.
7. Write any doctor's name that you know.

XVII. 1. Mr. Green's little boy has hurt his head. They have sent for Dr. King to attend him.
2. Miss Stone's pupils read and write very nicely.
3. Mrs. Sweet's three little boys are all very polite to everybody.
4. Mr. Mason's children are always very kind to each other.
5. Miss Smith's pupils have promised to be kind to animals.

XVIII. (Possessive of common nouns.)
1. The teacher's bell is on her desk.
2. The duck's foot is webbed.
3. The hen's head is small.
4. The boy's hat is lost.
5. The cat's fur is soft.
6. The dog's eyes are pretty.
7. The horse's mane is long.

XIX. (In dictating an exercise containing punctuation marks, the use of which has not been taught, the teacher should simply tell the pupil to put such a mark after such a word.)
1. One Wednesday in August Mr. Green took his three children down the river. While they were on deck, the wind blew George's hat off. He would have lost it if the captain's dog had not caught it and brought it back. The children were so pleased with the dog's sagacity that they begged Mr. Green to buy the dog. The captain

would not part with him, but told them that he could get them one like him in England.

XX. (A test.)
1. Henry's little sister was late at school last Friday.
2. We have no school in July and August.
3. When I came into school Wednesday morning, I found the teacher's bell on the floor.
4. Miss Stone began to teach in this building last December.
5. The baby's blocks are made of wood.
6. Have you ever been in Boston?
7. Would you like to live in New York?

## CHAPTER III.—THIRD YEAR.

### PRIMARY LANGUAGE TRAINING.

To tell stories well,
To report in a complete and orderly manner their observations,
To describe objects, tableaux, and pictures,
To repeat in their own language the substance of that which they have read, and
To write letters, correct in form and language and interesting in matter, are the five attainments in language to be secured by pupils during their first three years in school.

If they do each of these five things well, their training in language has been a success; so far as they fail in any of these points, their instruction has been a failure. The other exercises are preparatory to attaining facility and correctness in these.

Lessons in language have, or should have, a progress as orderly as lessons in number.

### CORRECTION OF ERRORS.

Each recitation may begin with the correction of ungrammatical expressions heard since the last recitation.

This may occupy one, two, or three minutes.

If a reply or a remark by a pupil contain a fault violating a principle not yet taught, correct the expression and proceed without comment. If the fault be one already discussed, call for its correction by the class.

### PRONUNCIATION.

An exercise in pronouncing selected words, dividing them into syllables, locating the accent, and giving the vowel sounds, may oc-

THIRD YEAR. 59

cupy three or four minutes. Teach marking of the vowels. Drill upon difficult combinations of consonants, final *d, t,* and *ing.*

This work may be joined with the work in reading or spelling, if the teacher prefers.

## Use of Grammatical Terms.

The grammatical terms, *noun, common, proper, singular, plural, adjective, adverb, pronoun,* can be sufficiently explained to third-year pupils to permit the teacher to use these terms freely in conversation, without asking the pupils to explain or define them, or even to use them themselves. When asked, pupils can often give a sentence containing a common noun, a proper noun, a singular noun, or a plural noun, although they could not have defined any of those terms. The practice helps them in selecting and defining the parts of speech later.

Observe that in the following lessons the use, the form, and the meaning of the thing taught occupies the body of the lesson. The technical term is not used until near the close of the lesson, and its use is not required of the pupils. The teacher uses it afterwards whenever convenient, and the idea becomes fixed by repeated association of the word with the thing, not by repetition of a definition.

## The Idea of the Sentence.

A matter of special importance, and likewise of serious difficulty, is to develop in every pupil a full and definite idea of a sentence. No definitions will do this. It can be secured only by the examination and construction of many sentences.

Let the teacher compose and write with her pupils, all joining in a common exercise. Let the exercise be a description, or better, a story. Let some one make the first statement. The teacher, selecting from several forms the best, writes it upon the blackboard, the pupils writing it upon their slates, telling what capitals and what marks of punctuation are used. Let this continue until the time or the subject is exhausted. The pupils have used a series of sentences. Fragmentary and redundant forms have been quietly rejected. Gradually the pupils discover the grounds of these selections and rejections, and the idea of the sentence has grown clearer to them.

## What to Teach in the Third Year.

1. The forms of the following irregular verbs should be learned during the third year: Begin, bite, blow, choose, cut, do, feed, forget, hang, hear, hold, keep, know, leave, lose, make, ride, ring, rise, send, set, sell, shake, shine, sing, sit, slide, speak, stand, strike, teach, tear, think, wear.

The irregular verbs taught during the second year [see p. 45] should be reviewed, and then the verbs of the list above should be studied in the same way, studying one new verb each week.

2. As often as practicable, pupils should write paragraphs reproducing stories or descriptions heard or read. (See Written Reproductions, p. 9.)

3. Once a week, or oftener, the pupils should write a paragraph or more giving an account of their observations or "nature studies."

The illustration which follows, p. 61, is supposed to have been written by the pupils as a summary of several paragraphs written at different times, as the facts stated have appeared. These paragraphs were prepared upon the plan mentioned under "The Idea of the Sentence," p. 59, and after all the facts had been learned the paragraphs were condensed and rewritten by the pupils as a composition exercise.

4. DICTATION EXERCISES. — At the beginning of the year the dictation exercises of the second year should be reviewed, and then the dictation exercises beginning on p. 81 should be taken. There should be frequent review exercises, and one new dictation exercise should be learned each week.

5. STUDY OF THE FORMS OF SPEECH. — Beginning on p. 62 will be found illustrative lessons showing how to teach the language forms that should be studied during this year.

The lessons are not supposed to cover the entire subject of language instruction for this year, but are designed to be suggestive of the method of treatment.

These lessons cannot be used just as given, for the simple reason that pupils will not always give just the answer that the teacher desires; yet if the teacher has made good preparation, and trains her pupils to answer just the question asked and not some other question like it, no difficulty beyond that of having to vary questions and introduce others will be experienced.

6. HOMONYMS.
7. LETTERS.

[A report by the pupils of observations of the growth of beans.]

### THE BEAN.

Our teacher put a bean into some cotton in a saucer, and Mary kept it moist by pouring a little water into the saucer every morning. After three days the bean split open at one end, and a little shoot came out. The shoot was smooth and white and curved upward a little at the end. Soon this end began to grow green, and two tiny leaves appeared. After a while a little bud came out between the leaves and stretched away from them. Then leaves grew on the end of this stalk, and so it kept growing on until it became a long stem.

The roots of the bean grew down, and other little roots grew out from them.

### HOMONYMS.

The sentences below may be written on the board, read, and copied by the pupils.

Ask them to find what word in each sentence sounds like one in the other sentence, but is not spelled the same.

Then direct them to use each of these words in a sentence of their own.

A bee is on the flower.
All the children must be good.

Mary is a dear little girl.
Near the pond stood a deer.

The girl is here.
The children can hear the birds sing.

Frank reads an hour a day.
Fannie does not live in our house

Henry has no book.
He will not know his lesson.

Kate always knows her lessons.
Kitty's nose is cold.

George does not know his lesson.
Go and untie the knot.

Susie has gone to meet her sister.
Lucy does not like meat.

I have learned my lesson.
I have a sore eye.

Julia can write well.
John made his tables all right.

Peter read his lesson.
Put the red ribbon on the doll.

Butter will melt in the sun.
Bertie is a very good son.

Robbie says there are no eggs in the nest.
Robins build their nests in the spring.

Our little girl goes to school to learn to read.
Olive wants to go, too.
One man and one man are two men.

Did you bring some wood for father?
Dannie would like to bring it.

As an illustration of a method of treating homonyms, the following exercise is given: —

### Eight — Ate.

1. Make the figure 8 on the board. Ask the children, "What did I do?" "You made an eight." Have the word *eight* spelled. Then show eight books, slates, pencils, marks, splints, or other convenient objects. "How many books are there?" "There are eight books." "Spell *eight*." "E-i-g-h-t, eight."

Dictate: —

Eight boys were playing ball.
There were eight apples in a dish.
Four books and four books are —— books.

## THIRD YEAR.

*Teacher.* What did you eat for dinner?
*Pupil.* I ate some meat.
Have this word *ate* spelled.
Dictate the sentence, I ate some meat.
Dictate : —
*Eight* tells how many there are.
*Ate* tells something you or some one else did.

The work upon homonyms can be extended at the discretion of the teacher. Except in reviews, not more than one pair or triplet of homonyms should be taken in one day.

The following, besides those given above, are suitable for this grade : —

| | | | | | |
|---|---|---|---|---|---|
| bear, | bare. | | sail, | sale. | |
| blew, | blue. | | see, | sea. | |
| by, | buy. | | sent, | cent. | |
| fore, | four. | | sense, | cents. | |
| flower, | flour. | | sew, | so, | sow. |
| grate, | great. | | stair, | stare. | |
| knew, | new. | | steal, | steel. | |
| lead, | led. | | threw, | through. | |
| made, | maid. | | wait, | weight. | |
| pail, | pale. | | way, | weigh. | |
| pain, | pane. | | wear, | ware. | |
| pair, | pear, | pare. | weak, | week. | |
| peace, | piece. | | whole, | hole. | |
| rose, | rows. | | won, | one. | |

### Lesson upon Nouns.

*Teacher.* What is this?
*Pupils.* That is an apple.
*T.* What is the name of this thing?
*P.* That is an eraser.
*T.* What is the name of this?
*P.* That is a table.
*T.* What is the name of this?
*P.* That is a desk, a book, etc.

*T.* What is your name?
*P.* My name is William Brown.

As the names are given write them in a column upon the blackboard. Ask the children to point to the thing of which *this* is the name. This. This.

*T.* How many names have I written upon the board.

Names are sometimes called nouns.

Write the word *nouns* upon the board.

How many *nouns* are in this column? In this?

## COMMON AND PROPER NOUNS

What is this? That is a boy.
Who is this? That is Willie.
What is this? That is a girl.
Who is this? That is Emma.

The words *child, scholar, teacher, man, woman,* with corresponding proper nouns, can all be brought out.

What is this road in front of the school called? (A street.) What street is it? What is the street a part of? (The city.) What city?

If in answer to the first questions about street and city, the proper names are given, accept them and ask, What is ——? (A street — a city.)

What body of water did you ever see (or is near here)? (Get both common and proper nouns.) What island can you mention?

As these words are obtained write them in two columns, proper nouns in one, common nouns in the other. Lead the children to observe that one of the columns contains nouns that can be used for all the objects of that kind, and the other, nouns which show which one in particular is meant. Let them tell which of two nouns that you give them can be used for any object like itself, and which one means a particular one. When they can do this, tell them that the one which can be used for any object of the same kind is a common noun, the one which is the name of a particular one is a proper noun. Let them discover that the proper nouns are all begun with capital letters. Tell them that proper nouns always do begin with capital letters.

## SINGULAR AND PLURAL NOUNS.

What is this? (An inkstand — a bell — a desk — etc.) When I say "inkstand," how many do I mean? What word should I use if I wished to speak of more than one inkstand? bell? chair? pear? cat?

(Use a number of examples, all having regularly formed plurals.) What is the difference in meaning between *cat* and *cats?* "*Cat* means one, and *cats* means more than one." Let them tell in this way the difference between several words, and then tell them that a noun which means one is a singular noun, a noun which means more than one is a plural noun.

Think of a singular noun. What is it? How do you know it is singular? Think of a plural noun. What is it? How do you know it is plural? Think of a noun either singular or plural. Which is it? How do you know?

What is the difference in the words *dog* and *dogs?* (*s.*) *Apple* and *apples?* Etc. How is the plural of most nouns made? Can you think of any not made so?

Man, woman, child, tooth, foot, ox, deer, sheep, leaf, knife, wife, mouse, goose.

The irregular plurals of these words should be written on the blackboard and learned by the pupils.

## POSSESSIVE OF SINGULAR NOUNS.

*Teacher.* Think of a common noun meaning a person.

(Receive several answers and write them on the board in a horizontal line like this: —

    boy       girl       cousin       uncle       etc.)

How many boys in this class?
How shall I write *boys?*
(Write it upon the board under *boy.*)
What is the difference in meaning between *boy* and *boys?*
Is this the boy's hat?
How shall I write *boy's?*

How many boys does that mean?
(Write it upon the board under *boys*.)
Use all the words of your blackboard list in the same manner.

The list will now appear as follows: —

| boy | girl | cousin | uncle | brother |
| boys | girls | cousins | uncles | brothers |
| boy's | girl's | cousin's | uncle's | brother's |
| | sister | aunt | father | mother |
| | sisters | aunts | fathers | mothers |
| | sister's | aunt's | father's | mother's |

Then ask, "When we add *s* to a singular noun, what does it make it mean?" (More than one.) When we add apostrophe and *s* to a singular noun it makes it show *whose* something is. When I say "The girl's hat," how many girls do I mean? How do I write *girl's?* When I say, "My cousins are coming," how many cousins do I mean? (Ask many questions like these, always adding, "How should I write ——?") What do we do to a noun to make it mean more than one? To make it show whose something is? We call the form of the noun which shows whose something is, the *possessive*.

## Possessive of Proper Nouns.

If John owns a sled, whose sled is it? To-day we will write the possessive form of some proper nouns. Answer all of my questions with some one's name.

Whose slate is broken?
Whose pencil is long?
Whose book is new?
Whose horse did you see?
Whose voice did I hear?
Whose book is torn? Etc., etc.

## Possessive of Plural Nouns.

You remember that the possessive form of a noun shows whose something is. What is the possessive form of *girl?* Put it in a sen-

## THIRD YEAR.

tence. Change the sentence to the plural. Make it mean more than one. How do you suppose we write that word *girls'*?

Obtain by questioning in the same way other regularly formed plurals. Write them all on the board, and see if they can tell you how to make the possessive of a plural noun. See that they *observe*, not guess. See if they can explain the difference in meaning between *girl, girls, girl's, girls'*, etc.

### POSSESSIVE OF IRREGULAR PLURALS.

In what do most plural nouns end? Do all plural nouns end in *s*? Think of some which do not. (Children, men, women, sheep, deer, oxen.) Write them on the board. Use one of these words in answer to these questions.

Whose slates are these?
Whose horses did you see?
Whose bonnets are in the hall?
Whose horns did you see? Etc.

After each question ask, "How do we write ——?" (poss. word), and write it. Do the same with some regular plurals.

How do we make the possessive of a plural noun? *Observe*.

### PRONOUNS.

[Review pronouns as taught in second grade.]

I.

he.

you.

she.
it.

John may stand — walk — write — look out of the window, etc. What are you doing? I am ——. Who is standing? I am standing. Ask another pupil, Who is standing? John is ——. What is John doing? He is ——. If pupil repeats *John*, tell him to use another word in place of *John*. Another pupil tell John what he is doing. You are standing. John, sit. Tell him what he was doing. (Look out for you *was* ——.)

Repeat with a girl; action different.

Henry, put your slate — book — anything — on your desk. Different pupils put different things on their desks. Where is the slate? The slate is ——. Use a word instead of *slate*. It ——. Where is the book? It ——. Etc.

When we talked about John, what word did we use instead of his name? When we talked about Mary? When we spoke to John? To Mary? When John and Mary spoke of themselves? When we talked about the slate, the desk, any object? As the pronouns are received this time, write them on the board. What did we use all these words instead of? (*Names.*) Words used instead of nouns are called pronouns. Write *pronouns* over the list.

Mary and I.
she and I.
we.

Henry, tell me that you and Mary were studying. Tell me the same thing, using a pronoun instead of Mary's name; the same thing, using only one pronoun which shall mean both of you. John, tell me the same thing about Henry and Mary, using their names; the same thing, using two pronouns; the same thing, using only one.

he and she.
they.

he and I.
we.
he and she.
they.

Lucy, tell me that you and Arthur like to play croquet; tell the same thing, using a pronoun instead of Arthur's name; the same thing, using one pronoun for both of you. Carrie, tell me the same thing about Arthur and Lucy, using two pronouns; using only one.

John, Carrie, and Bella may stand. What are you doing, Bella? Who else is standing? Who else? Tell me all of that in one sentence. John, Carrie, and I ——.

he, she, and I.
we.
they.

Tell me what you, John, and Carrie are doing, using three pronouns; using one. Another pupil tell me the same thing about John, Carrie, and Bella, using one pronoun.

you *were*.
*were* you.
you, he, and I.
we.

*Teacher* (*writing*). What am I doing? John, write; Eddie, write. John, what was I doing? Ask Eddie what he was doing. Eddie, ask John what he was doing. John, tell me what we were all doing, using three pronouns; using only one.

## OBJECTIVE PRONOUNS.

(Give book to boy.) What did I do? You gave me a book. To whom did I give a book? You gave the book to me. (Ask another pupil.) To whom did I give the book? You gave the book to John. Use a pronoun in place of *John*. You gave the book to him. (Repeat similar exercise with a girl — the action different.) Answer these questions, using no names; use pronouns instead of the nouns.

me.
him.
her.

me. Did I give a book to you?
him. Did I give a book to John?
her. Did I write a letter to Alice?

John, you may write your name on the board. Eddie may do the same. John, what did I tell you to do? Whom else did I tell to write? Tell me all of that in one sentence. (Eddie and me.) Tell the same thing, using two pronouns for you and Eddie; using one. Henry, what did I tell John and Eddie to do? Use a pronoun.

him and me.
us.
them.

(Show Lucy her own slate.) For whom was this slate bought? Show Lucy Carrie's slate. Ask Lucy the same question. Ask Lucy, "For whom were these slates bought?" (Carrie and me.) Use two pronouns for you and Carrie; use only one. Ask another pupil, "Were these slates bought for Carrie and Lucy?" Use one pronoun.

me.

her and me.
us.

them.

Henry may go into the hall and come back. Henry, whom did I send into the hall? Mary may go into the hall and come back. Henry, whom did I send into the hall? Use names in answer. Use two pronouns. Use one.

me.

her and me.
us.

him and her. Eddie, whom did I send into the hall? Use names.
them. Use two pronouns. Use only one.
you and me. John, ask Mary whom I sent into the hall. Use two
us. pronouns. Use one.
my sister and me. Tell me that your father wrote you and your sister
her and me. us. each a letter; use two pronouns; use only one.

| | |
|---|---|
| my brother and me. | Tell me that your mother gave you and your brother each a pair of skates; tell me with two pronouns; with only one. |
| him and me. us. | |
| him and her. them. | Tell me that I spoke to John and Susie, using two pronouns; using one. |

### Pronouns as Predicate Nominatives.

| | |
|---|---|
| | Pupils may answer, "It was ―――" or "It was not ―――," as they choose. |
| It was I. | Was it you whom I met last night? |
| It was not I. | Tell me that it was not you whom I met. ("'Twasn't me" is the commonest of all mistakes.) |
| It was he. | Was it George whom I heard talking? Repeat your answer, using a pronoun. |
| It was he. It was she. It was you. | Was it Henry who rang the bell? Repeat, using pronoun. Was it Mary who came in early? Was it I who gave you the book? (Be sure to receive "It was *not*," as often as "It was.") |
| she and I. It was we. It was he and I. It was we. It was he and she. It was they. | Tell me that it was you and Mary who saw the horse run away. Tell me the same thing, using two pronouns for you and Mary; using only one. Tell me that it was you and George who rang the bell; repeat with one pronoun. Tell me that it was Henry and Lucy whom I met; use two pronouns; use one pronoun. |

### Predicate Nominative with Present Tense of *To Be* in Dependent Clause.

Direct a pupil to stand. Ask, "Who is standing?" "I am standing." Teacher write "I     am standing," on board, with space between *I* and *am* large enough to write *who*. Ask, "Is it you who are standing?" Probably pupils will not say *am* in answer. Fill in the sentence on the board so that it reads, "It

| | |
|---|---|
| It is I who am. | is I who am standing." Ask a pupil not standing, |
| It is not I. | "Is it you who are standing?" Have a boy and a girl |
| It is not he. | stand. Is it George who is standing? Is it Eddie |
| It is he. | who is standing? Is it Carrie who is standing? Is it |
| It is she. | Lucy who is standing? Is it I who am standing? |
| It is not she. | Put "he ⸺ is," "she ⸺ is," "you ⸺ are," on |
| | the board, filling in as before, and show the pupils that |
| | the *who* does not change the word that we use with |
| | *I, he, she, you.* |
| It is I. | *Who is it who is writing?* Refer to yourself only in |
| It is he and I. | answer. Refer to yourself and George, using two pro- |
| It is we. | nouns; using only one. |
| | Ask another pupil, "Who is it who is ⸺?" |
| It is she and I. | (The action may be changed.) Refer to yourself and |
| It is we. | Mary in answer; use two pronouns; use only one. |
| It is he and she | Ask another pupil, changing the verb, "Who is it |
| who. | who is ⸺?" Refer to Henry and Lucy in your |
| It is they who. | answer; use two pronouns; use only one. |
| It is he, she, | "Who is it who is ⸺?" Refer to yourself, George, |
| and I. | and Mary in your answer; use three pronouns; use |
| It is we. | one. |

PREDICATE NOMINATIVE WITH **Was** AND **Were** IN DEPENDENT CLAUSE.

Ask questions similar to the preceding ones, using *was* instead of *is*. Obtain these answers: —

It was I who was ⸺.
It was not I who was ⸺.
It was he ⸺. It was she ⸺. It was you who were ⸺. It was he and I who were ⸺. It was she and I who were ⸺. It was we ⸺. It was they ⸺. It was he, she, and I ⸺.
Same exercise with *has* and *have*.

INTERROGATIVE PRONOUNS.

Direct the pupils to ask a question beginning with *who*. Receive a number. Pupils will be sure to begin some of these sentences with *who* and end them with *to, for, from, by,* etc. Teach them that a sentence must never begin with *who* and end with those words. If you tell them to begin that same sentence with *to, for,* or whatever word they finished with, they will change *who* to *whom* naturally.

Direct the children to ask a question beginning with *whom*. They will now begin to confuse *who* and *whom,* asking, "Whom did something." They will make mistakes which they wouldn't make in conversation, because they have just been saying "To whom," etc. Tell them that *whom* never does anything. Drill them in making questions beginning with *who,* with *whom,* with *to, for, from,* etc., followed by *whom.*

Direct the pupils to ask the question suggested by these statements : —

I gave a pencil to somebody.
Somebody came to see me.
I have bought a book for somebody.
Somebody is absent to-day.
I met somebody coming to school.
I took this book from some one.
This book was written by some one.
I saw some one writing.
I went away with somebody.

### Answers and Questions.

Of what question is this the answer, — I gave it to James?
[To whom did you give it?]

Ask me a question such that my answer will be, I bought it of John.
[From whom did you buy it?]

| Answers. | Questions. |
| --- | --- |
| I am going to town. | Where are you going? |
| John gave it to me. | Who gave it to you? |
| He went to the teacher. | To whom did he go? |
| He works for Mr. Brown. | For whom does he work? |
| It was done by Mary. | By whom was it done? |

# THIRD YEAR. 73

After the pupils become somewhat expert in finding questions to fit different answers, this form of questioning should be adopted whenever it proves the readier means of occasioning the use by the pupils of the forms you desire from them.

## ADJECTIVES.

What kind of day is it?
What kind of day is it sometimes?
What kind of article is sugar?
What kind of girl do we like? (Several adjectives.)
What kind of boy ought you to try to be? (Several adjectives.)
What kind of scholar fails to learn his lessons?
What kind of picture do we like?

Write the adjectives on the board, and ask the children what all these words tell. They will tell you "*what kind* something is." Tell them that a word that tells what kind something is, is an adjective.

Direct the pupils to finish these sentences with adjectives.

Apples are ———.
Henry is ———.
Flowers are ———.
That writing is ———.
That reading is ———.
That lady is ———.
That little girl is ———.
That boy is ———.
The weather is ———.

Pupils will often fill these blanks with nouns, as, Apples are fruit. Explain that they must fill it with an *adjective*, a word which tells what kind they are. Does fruit tell *what kind* the apples are, or *what* they are?

## COMPARISON OF ADJECTIVES.

Tell me something about this pencil, referring to its length. "That pencil is *short*." Tell me about the length of this pencil as compared with the one shown you first. "That pencil is *shorter* than the other." (Showing another still shorter.) Look at this one. (Putting all out of sight.) How many pencils have I shown you? Which of the three is this? "That is the *shortest*." Which of the three is this?

Repeat this exercise with other objects and obtain the superlative form of two or three more adjectives. (Thick, thin, heavy, light.) Write these superlatives on board. Then showing a small apple, say to the pupils, "Tell me about the size of this apple." "That apple is *small*." (Showing one still smaller.) Tell me about the size of this one compared with the other. "It is *smaller* than the other." (Put both out of sight.) How many apples did I show you? Which one is this? "That is the *smaller*." Which one is this? "That is the *larger*." (In another column write these comparatives.)

Mary and Carrie may stand. How does Mary compare in height with Carrie? "She is *taller* than Carrie." How does Carrie compare in height with Mary? "She is *shorter* than Mary." Which of those two girls is Mary? Refer to her height in answering. "Mary is the *taller*." (Write on board.)

Henry and Willie stand. Henry, how old are you? Willie, how old are you? Which of those two boys is Henry? Refer to his age in answering. "Henry is the *older*." Which is Willie? "Willie is the *younger*."

The teacher has often used the word *compare*. The children have not used it, but their replies show that they have understood it. The teacher can now call attention to the two lists on the board. How many things were we comparing when we used these words? (Two.) When we used these? (Three.) Take four or five pencils now, and ask, Which pencil is this? (Shortest or longest.) You see we use the same words when we compare three, four, or five — any number more than two, — and these words when we compare only two. Who can tell what change we make in the adjective when we compare two objects? More than two?

Make sentences in which you use the expressions, the sharper or the sharpest; the duller or the dullest; the brighter or the brightest; the quicker or the quickest; the prettier or the prettiest; the better or the best; the cleanest or the dirtiest, etc.

## This Kind — That Kind, etc.

Show several penholders of one kind in one hand, several of another kind in the other hand. Ask, How many kinds of penholders do you see? "I see two kinds." Which kind do you like better? Show several slates of each of two kinds. Which of these two kinds of slates is the more expensive? Which kind of pen do you prefer? (Always show more than one of a kind, so that if they are inclined to say "those kind," they may have an opportunity.) Tell them they must say "*That* kind," because even if there are several of the same kind, they are speaking of only one kind. Give a similar exercise, letting the pupils take the objects, to learn "*this* kind." Use the word *sort* with the same meaning. Tell me something about "*that* kind of."

## *Why* AND *What For.*

The distinction in meaning between *why*, which calls for the reason, and *what for*, which asks the purpose of an act, should be taught to the pupils as soon as they can readily suggest the proper question to secure a given answer.

This cannot be done without abundant illustration and careful analysis of the thought involved in the questions and answers employed.

Of this analysis, however, pupils of the third grade are entirely capable if they are carefully directed.

## *If* AND *Since.*

*If* implies doubt and precedes a supposition.
*Since* refers to a fact and prepares the way for a conclusion.
*If* 1 yard of cloth cost 6 cents, 5 yards will cost 30 cents.
*Since* there are 12 inches in 1 foot, in 10 feet there are 120 inches.

## *Less* AND *Fewer.*

Less = not so much.
Fewer = not so many.
Less money, sugar, cloth, time, etc.
Fewer apples, books, persons, pencils, etc.

## OPPOSITES.

*Teacher.* If you were going north and should turn about and go in the *opposite* direction, which way would you be going?
*Pupil.* I would be going *south.*
*T.* What is the opposite of north?
*P.* The opposite of north is south.
*T.* What is the opposite of east? What is the opposite of right? What is the opposite of left? What is the opposite of up? What is the opposite of forward? What is the opposite of top? What is the opposite of front?
*T.* Things may be opposite to each other in other ways than we have studied. *Hot* is the opposite of *cold ; wet* is the opposite of *dry.*

What is the opposite of smooth? Of large? Wide? Strong? Heavy?

Give the opposite of old, clear, light, right, wrong, poor, good, even, hard, tall, day, in, open, fresh, slow, solid, brittle, kind, brave, broad, polite, head, uncle, niece, healthy, land, sharp, stupid, first, deep, true, tame, asleep.

Use each of these words and its opposite in a sentence.

ILLUSTRATION: Iron is heavy. Feathers are light.

Let pupils combine these sentences, using such connections as the teacher suggests; as, —
Iron is heavy, but feathers are light.
Iron is heavy, while feathers are light.
Though iron is heavy, feathers are light.

## ADVERBS.

How am I walking? (Slowly.) How does Carrie recite? How does —— sing? How does —— read? How does —— recite? How should we behave? How should we speak? How should we study? work? play? talk?

Write on the board the words obtained in answer to these questions. These words all tell how something is done. Words which tell how something is done are *adverbs.* Words which tell what kind things are, are *adjectives*. A great many adjectives and adverbs are very much alike, as, John is a *rapid* walker, John walks *rapidly*. Many people make mistakes and use the adjective instead of the adverb. We must learn to be careful and use the right word.

What kind of girl does things neatly? How does a neat girl do things? John is a careful boy. How does he do things? John is a light sleeper. How does he sleep? Isabel is a rapid walker. How does she walk? Jennie is kind. How does she speak? George is polite. How does he treat people?

## The Senses.

What are our eyes for? What are our ears for? How do we know if anything is hard or soft? if anything is sweet or sour? if anything is fragrant or not? We find out all of those things by means of our *senses*. (Write *Senses* on the board.) We have five senses. Who can tell me what they are? Write, "hearing, seeing, smelling, tasting, and feeling," on the board.

How do flowers look?
How does music sound?
How does kerosene oil smell?
How does sugar taste?
How does iron feel?

In all your answers you used an adjective in answer to my questions. We have learned before that we use adverbs to tell how anything is done. We use adjectives to tell how things *look, sound, smell, taste,* and *feel*. If you think, you will see that those words don't tell how anything is done. The flowers, the music, the oil, the sugar, and the iron, are not doing anything.

How does the grass look? How does it look in hot, dry weather? (Dry, brown, withered.) How does a tiger look? How do flowers look? How does the sponge feel? How does silk feel? sand-paper? glue? Tell me anything that can be smelled. Tell me how any of those things smell. Tell me how something tastes.

## *Sit* AND *Set.*

Explain to the pupil that to sit means to rest: as, I sit upon a chair. From this as a model sentence obtain the forms, — You sit upon a chair. He sits upon a chair.

Then the past form, — I sat upon a chair yesterday. I have sat in my chair all the morning. He has sat in his seat all the morning. Etc.

Then define *set* as meaning *put* or *place*. I set the bell on the table. Develop the other forms.

Next have the pupil use the proper form of *sit* in each of the following sentences: The bell rests on the book. The boys rest on the bench. The bell has rested on the book for five minutes.

Then put the proper form of *set* into each of these sentences. I place the book upon the desk. John puts the ink-well on the stove. Mary has placed the chair on the platform. Thomas had placed the flowers on the desk before he came to class. Etc.

The next step will be to give many sentences with blanks to be filled by the pupil with forms of *sit* or *set*, as: The servant —— the table for dinner and —— the meat by father's plate. I —— the chair on the platform, and Thomas —— in it. I have —— in this seat for two weeks. I had —— it there before you told me.

Have pupils fill the blanks in the following sentences with the proper forms of *sit* and *set*. Notice what he says and —— it down in your note-book. —— still and study. I will —— a good example. His clothes —— very well. I will —— for my picture. Court —— next week. When the storm —— in, we were much afraid. Mary —— her hen on twelve eggs. He had —— on the doorstep until he was quite chilled. At four o'clock I shall have —— here two hours. They have —— on the bench since morning.

## *Lie* AND *Lay.*

Joseph, you may lay your pencil on the desk. What did I tell Joseph to do? What did he do? What has he done? What does he do with his pencil when he is not using it? What am I doing with this book? What do we do with our pencils when we are not using them? What did we do with our pencils this morning when we were through using them? What have we done with them now?

## THIRD YEAR.

What are the forms of *lay?* Spell *lay, lays, laying, laid.* To *lay* means to place or put down.

What was I doing with this book when I spoke about it before? (You were laying it upon the table.)

What is the book doing now? (The book is lying on the table.)

Carrie, do you lie down sometimes when you are tired? What shall we all do to-night? Carrie is tired; what ought she to do? We will suppose she has done it. What has she done? What did she do? What is this doll doing? Spell *lie, lay, lies, lying, lain.* To *lie* means to *remain, to rest.*

### TENSE.

*Teacher.* What do you see in this picture?

*Pupil.* I see a boy. I see a girl. I see a boat. I see some trees.

*T.* Do you remember what you saw on your way to school?

*P.* I saw a carriage with two men in it. I saw a man driving oxen.

*T.* What do you think you will see to-morrow?

*P.* To-morrow I shall see my father. To-morrow I shall see the parade. Etc.

*T.* What did you do this morning?

*P.* We ate our breakfasts. We came to school. We studied our lessons. We wrote on our slates. We read in our books. We helped mother with her work. We went to the store.

*T.* What will you do this afternoon?

*P.* We shall go home after school. We shall buy some candy to take to our little sisters. We shall ride in the street cars. Etc.

*T.* What would you do if you could?

*P.* If we could, we would clothe all the poor children that live in our town. If we could, we would earn so much money that our parents need not work.

*T.* What can you tell your folks that you have done to-day?

*P.* We can tell them that we have studied well. We can tell them that we have been good and kind. We can tell them that we have written our lessons. We can tell them that we have recited five times. We can tell them that we have seen the circus go past the schoolhouse.

*T.* What could you have told your mother last night that you had done yesterday?

*John.* Last night I could have told my mother that I had been at school all day. That I had reached the head of my class. That I had given Tommy a nice apple. That I had learned how to read a new lesson.

*T.* What do you think will have happened at your house before you get home to-night?

*P.* I think mother will have gotten supper ready for me before I get home. I think that father will have come home from Boston. I think that Aunt Mary will have come to see us. I think that Fido will have run away.

*T.* What may have been done with the ball this morning?

*P.* It may have been hidden. It may have been carried home by the owner. It may have been thrown behind the fence.

*T.* Who may have done these things?

*P.* Mary may have hidden it. John may have carried it home. Peter may have thrown it behind the fence.

*T.* What would you have done if you had been with Columbus when he first saw the red men?

*P.* If I had been with Columbus when he first saw the red men, I would have gone on shore with him to meet them. If I had been with Columbus when he first saw the red men, I would have kept close to the ship where they would not see me. Etc.

NOTE.— When pupils have become ready to answer questions using the appropriate form of the verb, they may be told to ask a question that has the word *run* in it, and to write the answer beginning with *Yes;* as, Can a dog run fast? Yes, he can run very fast. Many other verbs can be used in the same way. They may then be told to write a question beginning with *Did*, and containing the word *wring*, and then to write its answer. This will afford a very satisfactory drill upon past tenses. This work can be extended by using

*have* and some verbs named by the teacher.
*shall* and some verbs named by the teacher.
*had* and some verbs named by the teacher.
*can* and some verbs named by the teacher.
*may have* and some verbs named by the teacher.
*shall have* and some verbs named by the teacher. Etc., etc.

## DICTATION EXERCISES FOR THIRD YEAR.

### I.

(Review of Second Year. Statement, question, period, question mark, and the word *I*. This year call the question mark an interrogation point.)

1. Are you willing that I should take your book?
2. Many large plants and trees grow in warm countries.
3. Animals with fur live in cold countries.
4. Would you not like to visit other parts of the earth?
5. I would like to go to colder and to warmer countries.
6. I should see there different animals and plants from those I see here.

### II.

(Review use of capitals in names of persons and places, and use of caret and hyphen at end of line.)

1. Henry W. Longfellow was a famous American poet.
2. John G. Whittier is a poet who is now living in Massachusetts.
3. Longfellow and Whittier were both born in 1807.
4. The people of America love and admire both Longfellow and Whittier, not only for their poems, but for their beautiful character.

### III.

(Review use of capitals in names of days and months.)

1. The longest day of the year comes in June.
2. The shortest day of the year comes in December.
3. We go to school every day except Saturday and Sunday.
4. We go to church on Sunday.
5. I was in Boston one Wednesday last December.

### IV.

(Review possessive form of nouns in the singular.)

1. Last summer Henry's mother took him to Newport. They stayed in Newport through July and August.

2. These are my cousin's books.
3. My father's horse has hurt his foot.
4. Lucy's new dress is very pretty.
5. The cat's milk is in the saucer.

## V.

(Teach that the name of the person addressed is separated from the rest of the sentence by commas.)

1. George, will you bring me that book?
2. I think, Lizzie, that you must study that lesson again.
3. Do you think, Carrie, that you can finish that work by next Friday?
4. I should be much pleased, my dear Jennie, if you could visit me in New York.
5. I am sorry, John, that you did not succeed in your attempt.

## VI.

(Teach use of comma in a series of words.)

1. The sphere, cube, and cylinder are made of wood.
2. The cylinder will stand, roll, and slide.
3. I have a cloak, hat, scarf, and rubbers in the dressing-room.
4. George, Henry, and John are going to Chicago in September.
5. I have invited Louise, Alice, Susie, and Jennie to visit me next Thursday.

## VII.

1. The spring months are March, April, and May.
2. The summer months are June, July, and August.
3. The autumn months are September, October, and November.
4. The winter months are December, January, and February.
5. The days of the week are Sunday, Monday, Tuesday, Wednesday, Thursday, Friday, and Saturday.

## VIII.

1. London, Paris, Berlin, and New York are large cities.
2. France, Germany, Italy, and Spain are countries in Europe.

3. The United States, British America, and Mexico are countries in North America.
4. Rice, cotton, tobacco, and sugar-cane grow in warm countries.

### IX.

1. Trees have roots, trunks, branches, and leaves.
2. The four seasons are spring, summer, autumn, and winter.
3. The twelve months of the year are January, February, March, April, May, June, July, August, September, October, November, and December.

### X.

1. Can you, Jessie, tell me what you learned Monday about sponges?
2. In which city, Mary, would you prefer to live, in Boston or New York?
3. Do you think, Lucy, that George's little sister Carrie is very ill?
4. I think I would rather live in the country than live in any city.
5. The country is not so pleasant in winter as in July and August.

### XI.

(Teach the use of quotation marks, and that a quotation begins with a capital and is separated by a comma from the words which introduce it.)

1. Louise said, "Come, John, it is time to go to school."
2. Mother said, "Henry, will you go to the store for me?"
3. The captain answered, "We sail Saturday at four o'clock."
4. Jessie's mother replied, "I do not wish you to go to-day."
5. The man said, "I think it will storm to-morrow."

### XII.

(Teach the use of quotation marks with broken quotations.)

1. "Lawrence," said his mother, "have you finished your work?"
2. "I will go," said John, "as soon as I have read this chapter."
3. "Sponges and coral," said the teacher, "are obtained from the sea."

4. Grace's mother said, "Will you bring me your brother's coat?"
5. "Next Saturday," said Mary, " we will all go to Boston together."

### XIII.

(Teach how to write St. and Av.)
1. Mr. Smith's family live on State St.
2. Jennie and Susie are visiting friends on Madison Av.
3. There are many stores on Westminster St.
4. Do you not think Fifth Av. is pretty?
5. Will you go to Washington St. for me?

### XIV.

(Teach the use of apostrophe in contractions.)
1. John doesn't like to study.
2. Lucy hasn't any book.
3. I'll go if you will.
4. Shouldn't you think he would wish his teacher to love him?
5. He couldn't succeed in doing his work.

### XV.

(Teach the abbreviations Mr., Mrs., Dr., Mon., etc., Jan., etc., Capt., Col., Gen., Rev., Esq., ct., cts., doz., lb., pt., qt., pk., bu., gal., oz., M., P.M., A.M., and the word *o'clock*.)
1. Mon., Feb. 22, 5 o'clock P.M.
2. Tues., Jan. 12, 11 o'clock A.M.
3. Fri., Sept. 9, 12 o'clock M.
4. Col. Hopkins will be here next Saturday.
5. Capt. Jenks went to Boston last Wednesday.
6. Rev. Mr. Monroe will preach next Sunday.

### XVI.

(Teach form of possession of plural nouns.)
1. The girls' hats are in the dressing-room.
2. The boys' skates are in the entry.

3. Girls' shoes are not so heavy as boys'.
4. Men's hats are sold in this store.
5. Children's voices are very sweet.
6. Boys' sleds for sale here.

## XVII.

1. Ivory is obtained from elephants' tusks.
2. All of the boys will come early next Monday morning.
3. "Father," said John, "there is a store on Washington St. where they sell boys' skates for a dollar."
4. "Let us go into this store," said Miss Stone, "and look at ladies' hats."
5. I hope to see an improvement in the pupils' behavior.
6. The boys' manners are better than they were.

## XVIII.

(Letter forms. Teach how to write the address of a letter. Have the pupils write these addresses from dictation. A picture of an envelope could be made on the slate, and the address written in it. The address should occupy three lines. 1. Name of person addressed; 2. Street and number, if given; 3. City and state: or, 1. Name of person addressed; 2. Town or City; 3. State.)

1. Miss Mary Moore,
    425 Columbus Av.,
        Boston, Mass.

2. Mr. Charles Wall,
    280 Alexander Av.,
        New York City, N.Y.

3. Mrs. A. T. Sawyer,
    Colorado Springs,
        Colorado.

4. Address correctly a letter to your father or mother.
5. Address correctly a letter to your teacher.

## XIX.

(Teach how to write the heading of a letter. The heading has usually two lines, the first one telling where, the second when, the letter is written. Let the pupils copy these headings and afterwards write them from dictation.)

1. Boston, Mass.,
    July 16, 1890.
2. Philadelphia, Pa.,
    March 16, 1888.
3. 417 Broadway, Denver, Col.,
    Sept. 6, 1875.
4. Chicago, Illinois,
    Dec. 18, 1892.
5. Write the heading of a letter written from your home to-day.
6. Write the heading of a letter written from this school to-day.

## XX.

(The salutation of a letter to friend or relative is usually written on one line. Teach how to write salutation beginning with "My dear ——," beginning with "Dear ——," followed by either name or title, as sister, cousin, etc. Let the pupils write these salutations:—)

1. My dear Friend.
2. Dear George.
3. My dear Mother.
4. Dear Sister.
5. Dear Aunt Lizzie.
6. Dear Cousin Henry.
7. My dear Frank.
8. Write a salutation to one of your friends, using his name.

## XXI.

(The subscription of a letter includes the closing words of affection or respect, and the signature of the writer. It should be about as formal or informal as the salutation. To a friend or relative it usually expresses affection. Let the pupils write these subscriptions : —)

1.  Your affectionate son,
    Louis H. Williams.
2.  Your loving daughter,
    Carrie L. Morse.
3.  Your sincere friend,
    Frank Olney.
4.  With much love, from your cousin,
    Jessie Rogers.
5. Write a subscription for a letter from yourself to your father or mother.
6. Write a subscription for a letter from yourself to your teacher.

## XXII.

(Teach the position of heading, salutation, body of a letter, and the subscription. The first letter of the salutation fixes the position of the margin; the first letter of the body of the letter shows the indentation of the paragraphs.)

Write from dictation : —

NEWARK, N.J.,
Sept. 5, 1892.

MY DEAR NELLIE : —

We arrived at home safe Wednesday afternoon, and found father at the station waiting for us.

I am sure I never enjoyed a vacation so much before in my life, and Jessie says the same thing.

Do not forget that you have promised to return our visit at Thanksgiving time.

School begins next Monday.

Your sincere friend,
MINNIE J. NORTON.

## XXIII.

BOSTON, MASS.,
Feb. 16, 1890.

DEAR CHARLIE: —

Your picture came Saturday. I was very glad indeed to receive it, and thank you very much for it. It looks exactly like you, and I do not think that boys' pictures generally do look like them. Mother says that I can have some taken soon, and can send you one.

I would be very glad to receive a letter from you.

Your friend and playmate,
FRANK BROWN.

## XXIV. (Test.)

1. My brother's book is torn. 2. George's brothers are older than he. 3. My sisters live in the country. 4. The scholars' hats are in the dressing room. 5. Several girls are in the hall. 6. The boys have been playing ball. 7. The boys' jackets are warm.

## XXV. (Test.)

One Sunday, as Eddie and John were going to church, they discovered that John's dog was following them. "Will you wait for me while I take him home?" said John. "I will, if you will hurry," said Eddie. So John took the dog home and then rejoined Eddie.

## XXVI. (Test.)

1. I saw Henry, John, Lucy, and Carrie in New York, one Saturday last September.
2. "Are these the boys' books, mother?" asked Carrie.
3. The scholars' pencils all need to be sharpened.
4. Did you see many boys' skates in the store?
5. Ask the question suggested by this sentence: I saw somebody running.
6. Write the answer to this question: Whose book did you lay on my table?
7. Write the answer to this question: How long did you lie down?

# BOOK I.

This book is intended for pupils of the fourth, fifth, and sixth grades in schools having nine grades below the high school. In schools having a different grading it may be understood that this book is intended for the *middle third* of the grades below the high school.

### NOTES.

The Notes for Teachers at the end of the book should be carefully read before beginning the use of the book, and these notes should be referred to often as the class advances.

Suggestions for the treatment of many of the lessons are given in this Manual. It should be understood that the suggestions given are applicable to all similar lessons following. Some lessons may be omitted if a class be straitened for time. A few of these have been indicated. If a still greater reduction be found advisable, the work in description may be reduced and some of the reproductions omitted.

For the convenience of teachers the exercises in punctuation have been inserted in this Manual in their proper form. Teachers should not fail to emphasize the punctuation by requiring the explanation of the use of every mark in the punctuation exercises, and also by requiring the pupils to point out from the first the illustrations of the several rules for punctuation found in the reading, geography, and arithmetic lessons. In a short time the pupil will be able to explain the use of the greater portion of all the marks of punctuation that he finds, except the semicolon.

LESSON 1, p. 5. — Though such a lesson as this may apparently be quickly learned, it should be dwelt upon a few minutes on several successive days, and afterwards be referred to often.

L. 3. — See Description of Pictures, p. 10.

Lesson 5, and similar lessons, should be studied carefully, and each pupil be required to give numerous original sentences illustrating the use of each word. They should be briefly reviewed many times in class, but not assigned for review study.

L. 9. — At the time of recitation have a pupil read the first question, and secure answers from several pupils; then do the same with the second question, and so on. Several pupils may then describe the picture, looking at it, but not reading the questions. Finally, each member of the class may write upon his slate or paper a description of the picture. This will constitute the first recitation upon this lesson.

At the beginning of the second recitation let several pupils, some of the best and some of the poorest, copy their descriptions upon the blackboard. Let the class criticise and the teacher suggest improvements in arrangement and in form of sentences. The class may now rewrite their descriptions. While they are doing this, the teacher may render individual assistance as she passes from pupil to pupil. See note 7, p. 213, and note 12, p. 214, Book I. See also p. 10, Manual.

L. 14. — Dictation exercises may be copied in correct form by pupils and at a later exercise may be dictated. Every dictation exercise should be repeated once a fortnight or so, at unexpected times, until every pupil can write it without mistakes. Other dictation exercises involving the same principle should also be given. See Dictation Exercises, p. 53 and p. 81. After a class has studied its reading lesson or its geography lesson, some paragraph not before announced may be dictated. This will secure study and will test the ability of the class.

L. 17. — This lesson should be studied orally in class, one sentence at a time, each pupil taking a sentence; then each pupil may take a paragraph. This should be continued until the class can read it readily as a reading lesson. It may then be copied as rearranged, special attention being given to the paragraphing. A title should be selected, and the pupil should gain from this lesson a correct idea of the appearance on paper of a well-arranged and well-written composition.

BOOK I. 91

L. 18. — Encourage the pupils to give full, sensible, and original answers. They should be led to have contempt for the laziness that seeks to give the easiest answer that will be accepted.

L. 21. — Review lessons 2, 11, 13, and 20. Be very painstaking with this and similar lessons when they are first studied by the class. Each of these lessons may be used several times for unannounced reviews.

L. 22. — This is a particularly important lesson, as very few even among educated people pronounce all these words correctly. Drill first the ear to recognize the difference in sound between à and ä, and then by months of practice the tongue to utter these sounds in the words in which they are found. The lessons in pronunciation and homonyms have no connection with the other lessons, and may be taken up at convenience.

L. 25. — Review lessons 11, 13, 20, 24.

L. 26. — At the first writing, the children should answer the questions as directed. One or more of the exercises written in this manner may be copied upon the blackboard, and the class may discuss the combinations and improvements that may be introduced. The exercise should then be rewritten, not as put upon the board nor as amended by class criticism, but in as original and correct a form as possible. The object of the criticism of the composition upon the blackboard is not to give the children a set of sentences that they may copy, but to teach them how to criticise and improve their own work.

L. 27. — Pupils should orally, book in hand, make the variations in phraseology that are suggested. When the outline is put upon the board, the pupils should repeat the story from memory by the aid of the outline. If the words of the book are forgotten, so much the better. Correct inaccurate expressions in the oral work. The exercise should become familiar to the pupils before the written reproduction is attempted. Each pupil should reproduce the story in his own phraseology. No two reproductions of the class should be wholly alike.

L. 31. — Begin with the exercise at the close of this lesson. Copy it upon the blackboard as printed; have the pupils mention the first mistake, show them how to indicate the proper correction; have them find and read the paragraph in the lesson which tells how to correct such mistakes; and so proceed through the exercise. Then erase the corrected exercise and have it again copied as printed. The mistakes may be again pointed out, and pupils may be called to the board to indicate the proper correction as other pupils read to them the directions in the lesson. Next let each pupil, book in hand, copy the exercise as printed, and indicate the corrections. Again copy the exercise, and without the book indicate the corrections. This will be sufficient study of this lesson. Hereafter require the use of these marks as occasion offers, and if the pupil has forgotten them, let him refer to this lesson.

L. 35. — Can you fly like a bird? No, but I can run fast.
A boy can run and jump and play. A girl can read, sew, and sing.
Have you seen my new dress? Yes, I saw it yesterday.
Observe the three paragraphs, and the punctuation of the series.

Call the attention of the pupils to the paragraphs, and explain their use (see p. 84). Have pupils use the word *paragraph* as needed, without attempting, at this time, a definition.

L. 36. — Review lessons 24 and 30.

L. 43. — Review lesson 36. Have the pupils state all they notice about the punctuation and capitals, the margins, the paragraphs, and the position of each part of the letters in lessons 36 and 43.

Have the letters written upon slates from dictation, and several copied from the slates upon the blackboard; correct them by using the marks of correction taught in lesson 31. Notice the arrangement of the several parts of the letters. Dictate again and again, until every pupil can write them from dictation with entire correctness.

While this is being accomplished, lessons 44, 45, 46, 47, and 49 may be studied, and reviews may be taken of lessons not requiring written work in the recitation, or the correction of written work.

L. 48. — The questions in this lesson are serviceable only as suggestions leading the children to notice and think. Each pupil should select a title for his description. It will be well to talk about this lesson a few minutes, at two or three successive lessons, leading the children to play of imagination and original suggestions, before undertaking to write.

L. 49. — Another difficult lesson. See remarks on lesson 22.

L. 55. — Review lessons 37, 38, 54.

L. 56. — Review lessons 46, 47.

L. 58. — This lesson should be read many times at the beginning or close of recitations, when a minute or two of time can be found.

L. 63. — Has Willie a drum and fife? Yes, he has a drum, fife, and gun.

May I walk with you a little way? Yes, I shall be glad to have your company.

Dogs, cats, horses, and cows are domestic animals. Bears, wolves, foxes, and squirrels are wild animals.

The farmer raises wheat, corn, rye, and potatoes. Can you think of other things that are raised on a farm?

Why four paragraphs?

L. 65. — Review lessons 1, 6, 37, 38, 54, 55. While lessons 65, 66, and 68 are being studied and recited, let the class be thinking of lesson 67, and getting ready, by thought and conversation, to write one or both of the letters called for.

L. 69. — Barnum's great show is coming to our town in July. The animals are kept in cages. A man goes into the cage with the lion. Jumbo is dead. There are elephants, lions, tigers, hyenas, kangaroos, and gorillas in great number in Barnum's menagerie. Have you ever seen them? Yes, I saw them once.

L. 70. — Review lessons 24, 30.

L. 71. — Review lesson 11.

L. 79. — Have the description that your class writes of this picture copied and preserved.

L. 82. — The rule here given in respect to *O* and *Oh* is not one followed by all good writers, though it has the sanction of high authority. If your pupils follow it, they will not be led astray.

L. 83. — If the class has not time to write all three of the letters called for, let it write one or two of them. This remark may be understood as applying to all similar cases which follow.

L. 85. — May I go with you to see the hens?
Yes, I am going now. We must go to dinner at 12 o'clock.
When does the lecture begin?
At eight o'clock.
O Mary, it is time to go to school!
Where are my books? Oh, here they are!

L. 88. — The class should be able to take this lesson for a single recitation. At the recitation let each pupil read a question and give its answer. When this can be done very easily, let each pupil read silently several questions and give their answers.

Should the class be unable to do this readily, lessons 1, 6, 11, 13, 20, 24, 25, 30, 37, 38, 46, 47, 54, 55, 66, 84 should be reviewed, and then lesson 88 should be tried again.

L. 91. — The written description should be entirely apart from the story. The description and the story should be written upon different days, or the story will so overshadow the description that the latter will amount to very little. Make clear to the children the difference there is between description and narration.

L. 96. — Lessons 96, 97, and 98 should be taken up in the same recitation, read in class, and explained. The rules in lesson 98 may then be learned for the next recitation.

Hereafter, as long as the exercise is useful, have the rules of lesson 98 applied to the punctuation of the quotations found in the reading lessons.

When occasion arises, explain the use of the colon before a quotation. See Book II, p. 281.

L. 101. — The distinction between *rise* and *raise*, *sit* and *set*, or any other words likely to be confused, cannot be sufficiently taught in one lesson, nor in a dozen. The distinction must first be clearly perceived, and then afterwards referred to with additional exercises, it may be for years, until the *habit* of making the proper distinction becomes firmly established.

Lessons 102 and 103, with a review of lesson 95, should be taken for one recitation.

L. 105. — If teachers feel that too many forms for letters are given, and that the subject is treated in too much detail for their classes, lessons 105, 109, 110, 113, and 114 may be omitted, or used merely in part.

L. 106. — This description is given to be studied as a model. Let the pupils compare the several statements with the picture, then make an outline from the description or the study of the picture, and write another description.

Compare the description of this picture which your pupils write with the one they wrote of the picture in lesson 79. How much increased power of description do you discover?

L. 110. — Review lessons 24, 30, 92, 105, 109. After the letter forms have been studied and copied, they should be written from dictation.

Let the pupils see that much that has been said as to the arrangement of the parts of letters is merely a matter of taste, and can be accepted or rejected by any one who considers appearance and convenience. See note upon lesson 105.

L. 112. — The questions do not furnish an outline; they awaken thought. The pupil supplies the outline. The first demand at the bottom of the page is for a description of the scene in a general way. The second calls for a more detailed description of the pictures which the several pupils would paint, in illustration of the lines. The third is purely imaginative of a sitting-room in a humble German cottage. Nos. 2 and 3 may be omitted, if thought too difficult.

L. 114. — Review lessons 92, 105, 109, 110, 113.

L. 118. — Review lessons 20, 66.

L. 121. — Susan said, "Thank you, Aunt Kate, for my nice new book."

Her aunt replied, "I am glad you like it. Come and see me soon and bring your little dog. What do you call it?"

Jennie has taken her doll out for a ride in its little wagon. Her dog is running by her side. She says to him, "Jip, don't you run away."

Have the pupils give the reasons for the paragraphing, the rules for the marks of punctuation and the capitals. Dictate this lesson again and again, if need be, until it can be rapidly written without mistakes.

L. 122. — Lessons 122, 130, 135, 147, 153, 158, 168, 172, etc., deserve careful treatment, for they train the child's powers for description in a systematic manner. Their treatment should be mainly oral.

L. 126. — Review lessons 92, 105, 109, 110, 113, 114, 125.

L. 131. — Review lesson 116.

L. 134. — This lesson can be omitted if the teacher prefers.

L. 145. — Four boys in our school went fishing Saturday. Their names are Willie Stewart, Peter Smith, Jack Ray, and Moses Stade. Did they catch anything? O yes; they caught many perch, pickerel, and trout. Besides, they got their feet wet and caught cold.

L. 149. — Have Grace and Jennie got here yet?
No, not yet.
I am afraid they will be late. School begins at nine o'clock. Oh, here they come in their father's carriage.
Who is that in the carriage with them?
I think it must be their Aunt Susan who has come to spend Christmas with them.

Have the pupils arrange the paragraphs differently, and explain the difference in the meaning thus made.

L. 152. — Teachers who require their pupils to memorize definitions should have them learn the definition in this lesson rather than that in lesson 154. Teachers who desire pupils to phrase their own definitions will find assistance in both lessons.

L. 156. — Last Saturday our entire class went on a picnic.
Uncle Ned drove us over to the meadow in his long hay wagon.
How merry we all were!
There were five girls and four boys in our party.
Would you like to know their names? Well, here is the list: David, Edward, Robert, Joseph, Martha, Polly, Sarah, Nora, and little Maud.

L. 159. — Hasn't Frank gone home?
No, he has to stay after school.
Is Helen waiting for me?
Yes, she asked permission to wait till you came.
I am sorry, Helen, I kept you waiting so long. Miss Shaw, may we go now?
Yes, it is time for you to go.

L. 166. — Review lessons 152, 154, 157, 165.

L. 171. — O John, is it your ship?
Yes, it is my ship. See the flag.
Will the ship sail on the pond?
Yes, just as well as a big ship.
Will you go, Harry?
Yes.
Oh, I am so glad! Come with me.

L. 176. — Review lessons 95, 102, 103.

L. 181. — Review lessons 94, 97, 98.

L. 182. — Review lessons 13, 20, 103.

L. 201. — In last week's *Independent*, the Baptists are reported to be making great gains in the Southern States.
Can you give an account of the battle of Gettysburg?
To what address did you send the letter? I sent it to "Wm. Thompson, Esq., Thompsonville, Conn."
Have you had any reply? No, not yet. I don't expect any answer before Thanksgiving.
On what day of the week does Thanksgiving usually come? On Thursday.

L. 214. — Review lessons 152, 154, 166.

L. 218. — Review lessons 35, 82, 98.
London is in England, Berlin is in Germany, St. Petersburg is in Russia, and Washington is in the United States.
The cat said, "I'll catch you, little sparrow."
"No, you will not. I'll fly away," said the bird.
"Where are you going, my pretty maid?"
"I'm going to the meadow, sir," she said.

L. 223. — Review lessons 214, 215, 220.

L. 224. — Pupils may now have assigned to them for seat work the preparation of letters to the teacher, or to some other person, in which they criticise, in accordance with the suggestions of this lesson, the written exercises of their classmates.

The teacher should see that the work of criticism is carefully done, but may in this way be relieved of a great burden of work, while the pupils are much profited in undertaking it.

L. 227. — Review lesson 218.

L. 233. — Review lesson 229.

L. 234. — A sparrow caught a fly on the bough of a tree. The fly cried out, "Oh, dear sparrow; let me live, and go my way." "No," said the sparrow; "you must die, for I am great, and you are small."

L. 240. — An old miser had a tame jackdaw that used to steal pieces of money, and hide them in a hole. The cat saw him do this, and said, "Why do you hide those round, shining things, that are of no use to you?" "Why," said the jackdaw, "my master has a whole chest full of them, and makes no more use of them than I do."

L. 242. — Review lesson 236.

L. 249. — Review lessons 218, 244.

L. 256. — Peru, one of the largest states of South America, lies among the Andes. Palestine, or the Holy Land, lies along the east coast of the Mediterranean Sea. Egypt, one of the oldest countries in the world, is in the northeastern part of Africa. The capital of Turkey, Constantinople, is in Europe. Lisbon, the capital of Portugal, was once almost destroyed by an earthquake. Australia, the largest island of Oceanica, is often called a continent.

L. 258. — Review lessons 245, 248, 250, 254, 257.

L. 274. — Dictate this exercise until it is readily written by every pupil.

All the rules of punctuation usually needful for the punctuation of arithmetical solutions have now been taught (except the use of the semicolon in some instances, for which the teacher may give instruction as required). Have the pupils apply the principles of punctuation already taught to everything which they write, and often to explaining the use of the marks of punctuation found in the lessons in their text-books.

L. 292. — Review lessons 218, 244, 249, 264.

L. 297. — Greenland and Iceland belong to Denmark, and are called Danish America. The inhabitants of Iceland came first from Europe, and are a hearty, moral, and well educated people.

Look at this big, burly Irishman. He is tall and well made, and has strong arms for pulling the oars and hoisting the sails.

New York was settled by the Dutch, and was first called New Amsterdam by them in memory of their old home.

L. 312. — Clara had a little spot in the garden which she called all her own. She planted her flower-seeds in the spring, and watered and cared for the flowers all summer.

One day she was pulling up the weeds, when she saw her name written in green letters. Slowly she spelled it out. Who could have put it there?

"O mamma," she called, "do come and see my garden. See, there is my name growing right in the centre. Isn't it pretty? How did it ever grow that way, mamma?"

Her mother then said, "I planted the seeds in that way because I thought it would please you."

Clara was very glad her mother had done this for her. She took good care of the little plants.

L. 321. — Two or three of the more thoughtless among the boys were ready to laugh at him for stopping to help an old woman.

"It was but a little thing to do, boys," he answered, "and then, she is somebody's mother. Some one sometime may give a helping hand to my mother, if it ever happens that she's poor and old, and her own boy is far away."

The boys made no answer, for they felt that he was right.

# BOOK II.

If pupils have studied Book I, the earlier lessons in Book II will be in the main a review, and can be passed over rapidly. The remarks under the several lessons are intended to be applied not merely to the lesson under which they stand, but equally to all similar lessons that follow.

LESSON 2. — Review lesson 1. That a sentence be an imperative sentence, requires that it be in the imperative form as well as that it expresses a command, a wish, or a request. *I command you to do it* is not an imperative sentence; nor is *I wish you would come*, though the first expresses a command and the second a wish.

Do not raise such a difficulty with pupils, but be ready to give the explanation if the pupils require it. An exclamatory sentence is really a declarative, interrogative, or imperative sentence expressing strong feeling. It is put down as a "kind of sentence" because most grammarians so term it, and because it is more convenient to form and apply the rules of punctuation if it be so called.

L. 4. — The principle of punctuation that every figure, letter, word, or group of words, which represents a sentence should be followed by the terminal mark of that sentence, is an important one, and the illustrations of it, to be readily found in the pupils' text-books, should be pointed out.

L. 5. — Such a lesson is not to be learned and recited, but to be carefully read and comprehended. See that pupils think as they read it.

L. 7. — Review lessons 1, 2, 6.

L. 8. — Review lessons 3, 4.

## BOOK II.

L. 9. — Review lesson 5. If the work of the class suggests better topics let them be assigned instead of those named.

L. 10. — Review lessons 6, 7.

L. 13. — Review lessons 1, 2, 7, 10, 12.

L. 14. — Review lesson 8.

L. 16. — Review lessons 3, 4.

L. 17. — Such a lesson as this should be divided and taken, one topic at a time, while other lessons near it are being studied and recited.

L. 18. — Review lesson 15.

L. 19. — Review lesson 16.

L. 22. — As fast as the rules of punctuation are learned, they should be applied; first, to explain the use of the punctuation marks and capitals in paragraphs of the text-books; second, to the punctuation of gems, verses, maxims, and paragraphs containing valuable information or fine sentiment which the teacher may dictate; third, to the punctuation of the pupil's own papers.

In dictating for punctuation, the teacher should name the marks of punctuation which the pupil is unable to supply, and omit those which the knowledge of the pupils is sufficient to insert.

L. 23. — Review lessons 1, 2.

L. 24. — Review lesson 22.

L. 25. — See suggestions in Notes to Teachers. Also remarks on lesson 101, Book I.

L. 28. — See remarks on lesson 31, Book I.

L. 35. — Review lessons 7, 10, 12, 15, 18, 21, 23, 27, 31.

L. 36. — The list of compound words given should be taken, not as complete, but as illustrations of how similar words should be written. Do not commit the list to memory, but refer to it as occasion offers.

L. 27. — Review lesson 23.

L. 29. — Review lessons 22, 24.

L. 31. — Review lesson 27.

L. 34. — Review lesson 30.

L. 35. — Review lessons 6, 7, 10, 12, 15, 18, 21, 27, 31.

L. 38. — Try the lesson orally first, and discuss the advantages of different improvements that may be suggested. Have several pupils write the first paragraph upon the board, each according to his judgment, then compare, discuss, and decide. Do the same with the second paragraph.

If pupils write such sentences in any of their essays, — and they will be very likely to do it, — have them refer to this exercise for suggestions, and rewrite their work.

Lesson 39 will furnish material for several recitations. A method for the first lesson would be to send a pupil to the board to write the suggestions of the class as to what might be mentioned in the description of the horse. The class and teacher suggest points, and after agreement upon the form has been reached, the pupil at the board writes down the different suggestions. He thus prepares an outline similar in some respects to the first or the second outline given in the lesson. The class then decides upon the best order of those topics, and the pupil at the board rewrites them in this order.

Each pupil then writes upon his slate one, two, or more sentences upon each topic upon the board, taking them in order. Each pupil then combines, changes, and improves that which he has written, and rewrites it upon paper, in the best form of which he is capable. Some of the best of them should be copied upon the board, to form a model for others.

If the teacher will do this work himself, carefully and fully, two or three days before the class attempt it, he will be better prepared to guide the class in this work.

The description may be copied into a composition book, or placed on file for future reference. In four or five months from the first writing, have the class again write upon the same topic; and, after correction and copying, as was first done, let the two exercises be compared.

As often as once a month, a composition should be placed on file for future comparison, as above indicated.

## BOOK II. 103

L. 40. — Review lessons 12, 13.

L. 41. — After the class has mastered this lesson and the exercise in it, extend it, first, by giving several sentences to be analyzed, containing only subjects and predicates; second, by asking for several such sentences from each member of the class.

Do this with each lesson in analysis, being careful not to introduce elements not yet treated of.

L. 43. — Review lesson 40.

L. 44. — Review lesson 32.

L. 47. — Review lessons 15, 18.

L. 48. — After it has been corrected, have the description of the *bear* copied and preserved. See p. 65.

L. 49. — Review lessons 12, 13, 40, 43. That a verb is sometimes transitive and sometimes intransitive, according to its use, should now be shown by numerous examples. He *studies* grammar (transitive). He *studies* diligently (intransitive). This class reads very well. You may read lesson 45.

L. 50. — Review lessons 22, 24, 28, 44.

L. 51. — Review lessons 41, 47. If the teacher chooses to introduce with this lesson the adverbial element, which is marked with a line beneath it, as the adjective element is by a line above it (see lesson 91, p. 81), she will be able to select additional sentences for analysis with less difficulty, though the order of treatment will not be quite so logical.

L. 52. — Review lessons 8 and 14.

L. 54. — Review lessons 6 and 7.

L. 57. — Review lesson 52.

L. 59. — Review lessons 32, 36, 44, 50, 55.

L. 63. — It is a waste of time and energy to require pupils to commit to memory such lists as are in this lesson; but they should be able to state the facts as to the number of each noun in the lesson.

L. 66. — Spend a week, or two weeks, on this lesson, discussing the thoughts and their application. Show that several of the quotations mean very nearly the same thing; group them together; arrange the groups in good order for treatment; find the main thought in each group; state this thought in a short sentence; have every pupil copy these sentences upon paper, and with them at his hand, and the book laid aside, let him write as fully as he can upon True Politeness, making no quotations. While this is being done, other work in language, advance or review, should, of course, be in progress, and form a portion, greater or less, of every recitation.

The method of writing a composition outlined above is the method to which the pupil should become accustomed in his treatment of all abstract subjects; except that, of course, he usually deals with his own thoughts rather than with those furnished to his hand as here.

His method, then, will be: First, he will write down all the thoughts that occur to him upon the topic; second, he will investigate, read, converse, reflect upon the points upon which he wishes further light. At length he will begin the process which has been described in the directions for the treatment of this lesson.

The pupil should review this lesson every few months, treating it as freshly and fully as he is able, and comparing the result of his effort with what he had previously done.

L. 71. — Review lesson 67.

L. 74. — This lesson will afford suggestion of the proper method of treating such a subject. It should, of course, be given only at the proper season of the year. If the class has, unfortunately, had no training in such observational work, the lesson will be too difficult, and should be omitted.

So also lessons 80, 87, 93, 100.

L. 75. — Review lesson 72.

L. 78. — Review lessons 41, 47, 51, 75. Further sentences for analysis are the following: —

Take things always by the smooth handle. — *Jefferson.*
Education is the cheap defence of nations. — *Edmund Burke.*
In character, in manners, in style, in all things, the supreme excellence is simplicity. — *Longfellow.*

> Night, sable goddess, from her ebon throne,
> In rayless majesty now stretches forth
> Her leaden sceptre o'er a slumbering world.
> — *Young.*
>
> June is the pearl of our New England year.
> . . . Long she lies in wait,
> Makes many a feint, peeps forth, draws coyly back,
> Then from some southern ambush in the sky,
> With one great gush of blossoms storms the world.
> — *Lowell.*

L. 81. — Review lesson 47.

L. 85. — Review lessons 27, 49.

L. 86. — Review lesson 51.

L. 89. — Review lessons 67, 71, 72, 75, 85.

L. 91. — Review lesson 21.

L. 94. — Review lessons 12, 13, 40, 49, 85.

L. 96. — Review lesson 90.

L. 98. — Review lessons 85, 94.

L. 103. — Review lessons 90, 96.

L. 105. — Review lessons 40, 85, 94.

L. 107. — Review lessons 90, 96, and 103. Require pupils to point out illustrations of the statements of these lessons in their reading lessons.

L. 109. — Review lessons 23, 47.

L. 112. — Review lessons 44, 75, 76.

L. 115. — Review lesson 91.

L. 118. — Review lesson 112.

L. 120. — Pupils should take pains with reproductions, not to repeat as nearly as may be the language of the work, nor yet simply to give the thought; but to give the thought in the fullest and most pleasing manner of which they are capable.

"You should submit to the judgment of your pupils various schemes of possible arrangement and gradually make them feel the superiority of some to others, while there may be occasions where the reasons are equally balanced. I do not know any exercise, within the compass of grammar, more profitable than this. It no doubt rises beyond grammar into considerations commonly included in rhetoric." — ALEXANDER BAIN, *On Teaching English*, p. 6.

L. 125. — Review lesson 49.

L. 131. — Review lessons 125, 129.

L. 132. — Review lesson 122.

L. 135. — Review lesson 112.

L. 141. — Review lesson 137.

L. 142. — Learn this lesson so that when any irregular verb is named its principal parts and class can be given.

L. 143. — Review lessons 76, 122, 126, 132.

L. 152. — Review lessons 90, 96.

L. 154. — Review lessons 54, 135.

L. 155. — Review lesson 22.

L. 158. — Review any lessons upon punctuation not fully fixed in the pupils' minds.

L. 162. — Review lessons 10, 112, 121, 147.

L. 166. — The study of the regular conjugations of the verb is divided into several lessons, in which the subject is treated in a new and helpful order. In lesson 166 the pupil learns the present tense of *shall* and *will*, and the form of arrangement of a tense in conjugation. In lesson 172 he learns the conjugation of *may* with its past tense *might*. These two preliminary lessons on the auxiliaries being learned, the pupil is able in lesson 176 to give the entire conjugation of *have*. He learns the present tense and the past tense of this verb. The future tense is simply *have* joined to *shall* and *will*, already learned. The remaining three tenses of the indicative are formed from the three just given by simply adding *had*. The present and past potential are formed by adding *have* to the forms of *may* already learned, and the present perfect and past perfect by adding *had* to these forms.

No advance beyond lesson 176 should be made until each pupil can easily repeat or write every part of the conjugation of the verb *have*.

L. 167. — Review lessons 152, 157. The following stanza from Longfellow is a model of good arrangement of adverbial and adjective modifiers with an emphatic subject: —

In the Old Colony days, in Plymouth, the land of the Pilgrims,
To and fro, in a room of his simple and primitive dwelling,
Clad in doublet and hose, and boots of Cordovan leather,
Strode with a martial air Miles Standish, the Puritan Captain.

It may be used for analysis and parsing.

L. 168. — The proper officer of the bank upon which a check is drawn may "certify" it by writing his name across the face of the check under the word *good* or some customary equivalent. A check so treated is called a "certified check."

Have pupils prepare checks payable to A——, B——, or bearer, and "certify" them.

L. 172. — Review lesson 166.

L. 174. — Review lesson 168. Notes and drafts (see lessons 182 and 197) are endorsed in the same way and with the same effect as checks. Each person who endorses a check, note, or draft guarantees its payment unless he writes above his name "without recourse," in which case he simply transfers his title or interest but does not guarantee the payment.

L. 176. — Review lessons 166, 172.

L. 179. — Review lessons 166, 172, 176. Do not attempt this lesson until lesson 176 is thoroughly familiar.

L. 180. — Review lessons 90, 96, 107.

L. 184. — This lesson must be made thoroughly familiar by daily reviews.

L. 185. — Review lesson 180.

L. 187. — Review lessons 129, 131.

L. 189. — Review lessons, 15, 40.

L. 196. — Review lesson 193.

L. 198. — Review lessons 193, 196.

L. 202. — Review lesson 166.

L. 203. — Review lessons 145, 159, 168, 174, 182, 191, 197.

L. 205. — Review lesson 167.

L. 206. — Review lessons 166, 172, 176, 179, 184, 193.

Review lessons 196, 198, 202.

L. 209. — Now or soon, let the pupils turn back to lesson 144, and write it again. They should not write again what they wrote before, but should see how much better they are now capable of doing than they then were. A test of this kind should be made once a quarter, or oftener.

L. 211. — Review lessons 145, 182, 197.

L. 215. — Review lesson 210.

L. 218. — Review lessons 12, 49, 125, 129, 131.

L. 225. — A lesson like this should be divided up and taken piecemeal in connection with reviews or lessons requiring composition.

L. 234. — Review lesson 230.

L. 236. — Have the following beautiful description by Longfellow of a summer's morning copied upon the board. Have the pupils study it until they feel its beauty, then lead them to take the further step and find in what the secret of its beauty lies.

Can they find any beautiful paragraphs in their reader, whose beauty springs from the same source?

<blockquote>
The village of Plymouth
Woke from its sleep, and arose, intent on its manifold labors.
Sweet was the air and soft; and slowly the smoke from the chimneys
Rose over roofs of thatch, and steadily pointed eastward.
Merrily sang the birds, and the tender voices of women
Consecrated with hymns the common cares of the household.
Out of the sea rose the sun, and the billows rejoiced at his coming;
</blockquote>

BOOK II. 109

Beautiful were his feet on the purple tops of the mountains;
Beautiful on the sails of the *Mayflower* riding at anchor.
— *Courtship of Miles Standish.*

L. 241. — Review lessons 51, 82, 86.

L. 245. — Review lesson 154.

L. 247. — Review lesson 242.

L. 248. — Review lessons 154, 245.

L. 253. — Review lessons 23, 31.

L. 257. — Review lessons 242, 252.

L. 261. — The study of metaphor should be continued incidentally for many months. The pupils should be required to select and explain all the metaphors found in their reading lessons. They should also be encouraged to bring to class examples of striking and pleasing metaphors found in their other reading.

L. 262. — Review lesson 259.

L. 267. — Review lessons 23, 253.

L. 272. — Review lesson 254. Additional sentences for practice may be found below: —

Thou art master of thy unspoken word; thy spoken word is master of thee. — *Anonymous.*

A soft answer turneth away wrath, but grievous words stir up anger. — *Proverbs.*

This was the wedding morn of Priscilla, the Puritan maiden, and her friends were assembled together.

Guard well thy thoughts; our thoughts are heard in heaven. — *Young.*

    The day is done, and slowly from the scene,
    The stooping sun upgathers his spent shafts,
    And puts them back into his golden quiver.
                              — *Longfellow.*

    The splendor falls on castle walls,
    And snowy summits old in story,
    The long light shakes across the lakes,
    And the wild cataracts leap in glory.
                                — *Tennyson.*

Now came still evening on, and twilight gray
Had in her sober livery all things clad.
— *Milton.*

The noble stag was pausing now,
Upon the mountain's rugged brow.
With anxious eye, he wandered o'er
Mountain and meadow, moss and moor.
— *Scott.*

A traveller through a dusty road,
Strewed acorns on the lea;
And one took root, and sprouted up,
And grew into a tree.
— *Mackay.*

All things above were bright and fair,
All things were glad and free;
Lithe squirrels darted here and there,
And wild birds filled the echoing air
With songs of liberty.
— *Anonymous.*

Within the fisherman's cottage,
Is shining a ruddy light;
And a little face at the window
Peers out into the night.
— *Anonymous.*

The old house by the lindens
Stood silent in the shade,
And on the gravelled pathway
The light and shadow played.
— *Longfellow.*

L. 275. — Review lesson 271.

L. 276. — Review lessons 253, 267.

L. 278. — Review lessons 254, 272.

L. 280. — Review lessons 273, 277.

L. 285. — Sentences 1, 2, and 4 are periodic; 3, 5, and 6 loose.

L. 287. — Review lessons 276, 278.

L. 292. — Review lessons 273, 277, 280, 286.

L. 304. — Review lessons 294, 296, 300.

L. 309. — Additional sentences.

> The day is drawing to a close,
> And what good deed since first it rose,
> Have I presented, Lord, to Thee,
> As offerings of my ministry?
> What wrongs repressed, what right maintained,
> What struggle passed, what victory gained,
> What good attempted, and attained?
> Feeble, at best, is my endeavor!
> I see, but cannot reach the height
> That lies forever in the light,
> And yet, forever and forever,
> When seeming just within my grasp,
> I feel my feeble hands unclasp
> And sink discouraged into night!
> For Thine own purpose Thou hast sent
> This strife and this discouragement.
> — *The Golden Legend.*

Every inmost aspiration is God's angel undefiled,
And in every "O my father!" slumbers deep a "Here, my child."

L. 313. — Review lesson 160.

L. 326. — Require the pupil to refer to the rule for each capital and mark of punctuation. Study the exercise until this can be done quickly and correctly.

www.ingramcontent.com/pod-product-compliance
Lightning Source LLC
Chambersburg PA
CBHW020137170426
43199CB00010B/782